ESSENTIAL PRAYERS FOR THE DEAD

ESSENTIAL PRAYERS FOR THE DEAD

Written and compiled by

Mary Leonora Wilson, FSP

Pauline
BOOKS & MEDIA
BOSTON

Nihil Obstat: Reverend Joseph Briody, S.S.L., S.T.D

Imprimatur: ✠ Seán P. Cardinal O'Malley, O.F.M. Cap.
Archbishop of Boston
December 20, 2023

Library of Congress Control Number: 2023951458

ISBN 10: 0-8198-8385-9
ISBN 13: 978-0-8198-8385-8

Cover art by www.kenjames.studio

Published by Pauline Books & Media, 50 Saint Paul's Avenue, Boston, MA 02130–3491

Printed in USA.

www.pauline.org

Pauline Books & Media is the publishing house of the Daughters of St. Paul, an international congregation of women religious serving the Church with the communications media.

1 2 3 4 5 6 7 8 9 28 27 26 25 24

"I am the resurrection and the life.
Those who believe in me,
even though they die, will live."

John 11:25

Contents

Introduction

While I learned to pray for the dead early in life, it is only since the death of my father twenty-five years ago that I have experienced a real connection with those who have died. My father was a good man and I loved him dearly. He was generous in his practice of charity and good deeds (most of which we discovered after his death). Of course, he had his faults—his temper, his issues with society and with the Church—but he served his country, loved his family, and had a compassionate heart. His sudden passing was a great loss, taking all of us off guard.

My mother was probably the most affected. Our large family home, filled with furniture my dad had made and the memories they had shared, became too overwhelming. Mom felt the need to move to a smaller house, something that she could manage on her own, one that wouldn't constantly remind her of her loss. She turned to me, her oldest child, to help.

Since I joined the convent at a rather young age, I had no experience in selling or buying houses. One of my younger brothers put us in contact with a real estate agent, which was very helpful but did not entirely relieve me of my feelings of inexperience and insecurity. I decided to entrust the whole thing to Dad, for whose soul I had been praying.

Our family home was put on the market, and open house was on a Sunday. The realtor arrived and Mom and I left for Mass. As we drove past the "For Sale" sign, I silently prayed the Eternal Rest prayer for Dad and added, "Please, sell this house quickly. It's really hard on Mom." I offered my Mass for Dad, thinking that he was probably in purgatory and wanting him to enjoy heaven as soon as possible. After Mass we went for breakfast and then headed back to the house. The first thing I noticed was that the "For Sale" sign was gone. Was it possible? We had been away for barely two hours! Sure enough, in the first hour (the hour of the Mass) we had three potential buyers. Mom chose to sell to a widow who was taking in her daughter and grandchild and needed a bigger house. Not only did the widow want to buy, but she also accepted our selling price. The whole experience was amazing and spoke to me on so many levels: God's divine providence, the fact that my father was in a position to intercede for us, the communion between ourselves and our departed, and the power of trustful prayer.

Situations like this happened repeatedly in the days to come as well as in the years that followed: the presence of and connection with departed relatives and friends; the consolation of being able to assist them with prayer and good works; the experience of their intercession in my own needs, spiritual and temporal.

This book is a tribute to all who have gone before us, living this pilgrimage called life to the best of their ability, not perfectly but sincerely and full of hope in the promise of our risen Lord and Savior, Jesus Christ. It is a booklet for all who mourn a loss and want to continue to help their loved ones and experience their nearness. May these texts and prayers help you to draw closer to those who have died and increase your faith in the resurrection of the dead and in the loving mercy of God. God bless you.

Mary Leonora Wilson, FSP

I

Purgatory En Route to Heaven

> Here we have no lasting city, but we are looking for the city that is to come.
>
> —*Hebrews 13:14*

What Happens When We Die?

Is the present reality all there is to life? Are my deceased loved ones gone forever? Or is life changed, continuing in some other form? These are questions that have resurfaced in every age since the beginning of recorded history. Our Catholic faith assures us that the answer to these questions lies in the deeper reality that we are indeed created by God with an immortal soul destined to live forever. Sacred

Scripture reminds us of this repeatedly. Jesus' own resurrection from death is the ultimate proof of this truth. Didn't he say, "I go to prepare a place for you . . . so that where I am, there you may be also" (Jn 14:2–3)? How consoling and encouraging these words are! To live with Jesus forever—this is heaven! And it means that we, too, will pass through death into life. Saint Paul expresses it eloquently and somewhat dramatically: "We will all be changed, in a moment, in the twinkling of an eye, at the last trumpet. . . . For this perishable body must put on imperishability, and this mortal body must put on immortality" (1 Cor 15:51–53). The change begins at death when soul and body are separated. Then, when time ends, both body and soul will be reunited at the final resurrection.

Scripture tells us that those who love God will inherit eternal life, but those who hate and reject God will go to eternal damnation. Yet for some there might arise a gnawing uncertainty: What if the person who dies is good but not good enough for heaven? Doesn't Sacred Scripture say that nothing imperfect or unclean can enter heaven (see Rev 21:27)? Instinctively we know that what is sin-stained cannot remain in the all-holy presence of God. And even when we have been baptized into Christ's death and saved through his redemption, repeatedly washed in the sacrament of Reconciliation, still there may be certain attachments to sinful habits that we have not given up. As this is true for us, so it could be true for our loved ones who have died. They may not have known Jesus Christ or practiced the Christian faith perfectly, but they did not reject God and they tried to live a good and upright life. The Church teaches that *all* who die in God's friendship are saved through the death and resurrection of Jesus Christ (see CCC 1260). But to enter that holy state of heavenly joy, the deceased need to be purified of anything that mars the divine image in them (see CCC 1030). Our very reason points to the logic of this.

God, who is love and mercy, is merciful to the very end and provides all who long for him the opportunity to purify and perfect themselves *even after this earthly life*. This is part of the grace won for us by the death and resurrection of Jesus Christ. This state of purification the Catholic Church calls *purgatory*, deriving from a Latin verb *purgare*, meaning "to cleanse." It's important for us to understand this aspect of salvific discipline as part of God's mercy and love. Reading Hebrews 12:9–10 in this light could prove very helpful: "We had human parents to discipline us, and we respected them. Should we not be even more willing to be subject to the Father . . . ? For . . . he disciplines us for our good, in order that we may share his holiness." The aim of purgatory is precisely this—to achieve holiness.

What Does the Bible Say About Purgatory?

The word "purgatory" as such is not found in the Bible, but references to a state of purification are.

One important Scripture text in our understanding of purgatory comes to us from Saint Paul, who speaks in metaphors of the judgment and purification of the Christian after death:

> For no one can lay any foundation other than the one that has been laid; that foundation is Jesus Christ. Now if anyone builds on the foundation with gold, silver, precious stones, wood, hay, straw—the work of each builder will become visible, for the Day will disclose it, because it will be revealed with fire, and the fire will test what sort of work each has done. If what has been built on the foundation survives, the builder will receive a

> reward. If the work is burned, the builder will suffer loss; the builder will be saved, but only as through fire. (1 Cor 3:11–15)

The foundation of our lives is Jesus Christ. The building we construct (i.e., our earthly life) can be made of any number of materials—some of them worthy and precious, some of them not; these are our works. Those works that fall short of our Christian calling, Saint Paul says, will be burned up, and he adds: "*the builder will be saved, but only as through fire.*" Here we have the imagery of refining fire that is so often associated with purgatory.

Pope Benedict XVI, in his encyclical *Spe Salvi* (Saved in Hope), offers a beautiful commentary on this passage and then goes on to say:

> Some recent theologians are of the opinion that the fire which both burns and saves is Christ himself, the Judge and Savior. The encounter with him is the decisive act of judgement. Before his gaze all falsehood melts away. This encounter with him, as it burns us, transforms and frees us, allowing us to become truly ourselves. All that we build during our lives can prove to be mere straw, pure bluster, and it collapses. Yet in the pain of this encounter, when the impurity and sickness of our lives become

> evident to us, there lies salvation. His gaze, the touch of his heart heals us through an undeniably painful transformation "as through fire". But it is a blessed pain, in which the holy power of his love sears through us like a flame, enabling us to become totally ourselves and thus totally of God. In this way the inter-relation between justice and grace also becomes clear: the way we live our lives is not immaterial, but our defilement does not stain us forever if we have at least continued to reach out towards Christ, towards truth and towards love. Indeed, it has already been burned away through Christ's Passion. At the moment of judgment we experience and we absorb the overwhelming power of his love over all the evil in the world and in ourselves. The pain of love becomes our salvation and our joy.[1]

We understand purgatory as an intermediate state between this earthly life and eternal life with God where those who have died in God's grace but still wounded by sin are fully healed, purified, and made holy for heaven. It is a state of perfecting in love, the result of God's infinite love and mercy. *Love* is the key to a right understanding of purgatory. Those who are in purgatory have seen him in a moment of personal judgment after death, have understood that God is their all, and have been filled with a deep, ardent love and a longing to be made worthy of the Lord through purification. While the pain of purgatory is real, it is a pain born of love. Those in purgatory love God, know that they are saved, and know that their suffering is temporary, preparing them for a life of eternal happiness with God, their Beloved.

Why Is It Important to Pray for the Dead?

Scripture lets us understand that it's important to pray for those who have died. In the Second Book of Maccabees, Judas Maccabeus takes up a collection as a sin offering for fallen soldiers under his command and the Scripture writer comments:

> In doing this he acted very well and honorably, taking account of the resurrection. For if he were not expecting that those who had fallen would rise again, it would have been superfluous and foolish to pray for the dead. But if he was looking to the splendid reward that is laid up for those who fall asleep in godliness, it was a holy and pious thought. Therefore he made atonement for the dead, so that

> they might be delivered from their sin. (2 Mac 12:43b–45)

Through prayer, intercession can be made in Jesus' name for the sins of the dead to help shorten their time of purification. Thus, they not only receive comfort and refreshment through our prayer, but their entrance into heaven is hastened as well. When someone we love is in need, we try to do everything in our power to help, being there for our loved one to the best of our ability. And while it is true that we can no longer help our departed family members and friends materially, God has given us the power to help them spiritually—the power of prayer—and he wants us to use that power. How encouraging are the words of Jesus: "I will do whatever you ask in my name" (Jn 14:13).

II

Helping Those Who Have Died

> Happy are those who consider the poor.
>
> —*Psalm 41:1*

As sons and daughters of God and brothers and sisters of Jesus Christ, we are all intrinsically connected with one another as part of God's family. That relationship doesn't end with this mortal sojourn but continues into eternity. Those who have died as friends of God, even though not visible to us, are present and living; it is the promise of Jesus: "I am the resurrection and the life. Those who believe in me, even though they die, will live" (Jn 11:25). This consoling truth is also an invitation to continue to nurture our relationship with the deceased through prayer and works of charity. They will most certainly reciprocate by praying for us as well.

Twelve Ways to Help Our Beloved Dead

1. Devoutly participate in Holy Mass for the deceased and have Masses said for your departed loved ones, especially on the anniversary of their death.
2. Receive Holy Communion as a prayer for the deceased.
3. Make a visit to the Blessed Sacrament on their behalf.
4. Pray the Rosary for their liberation.
5. Make the Stations of the Cross for their purification.
6. Pray the Divine Mercy Chaplet for the departed.
7. Pray a novena for the Holy Souls.
8. Practice small acts of self-denial for those in purgatory.
9. Give alms and do acts of charity as an offering for the dead (see Tob 12:9).
10. Ask the saints to join you in interceding for the faithful departed.

11. When passing a cemetery, pray the Eternal Rest prayer.
12. Gain indulgences for the deceased. On all the days from November 1 to November 8, a plenary indulgence, applicable only to the Poor Souls, is granted to those who visit a cemetery and pray for the departed (see page 19 for the requirements regarding indulgences). Partial indulgences are granted to those who recite Lauds or Vespers of the Office of the Dead,[2] and to those who recite the Eternal Rest prayer.

The Holy Sacrifice of the Mass

The greatest prayer, and the one that helps the souls in purgatory the most, is the Holy Sacrifice of the Mass. At the Mass, the sacrificial memorial of Jesus Christ takes place on the altar, and the work of the redemption is renewed each time it is celebrated. "In the Eucharist Christ gives us the very body which he gave up for us on the cross, the very blood which he 'poured out for many for the forgiveness of sins'" (CCC 1365). There is no greater prayer and nothing more precious or pleasing to God the Father than offering the Sacrifice that his Son made on Calvary. And because it is this Sacrifice that opened the gates of heaven for us, it is also the greatest gift we can offer for the relief and liberation of the souls in purgatory.

To offer Masses for the dead is one of the best ways to show our love for them. There are many opportunities available: participating at Mass on behalf of persons who have died and praying for them, having Masses offered by a priest for the deceased, enrolling the deceased in perpetual Masses (available from most religious congregations), or having the thirty Gregorian Masses celebrated for a loved one who has died. The Gregorian Masses are a series of thirty Masses offered on thirty consecutive days for the soul of one individual person. The custom originated with Saint Gregory the Great and is believed to be one of the most efficacious means for delivering a soul from purgatory.

It's important to pray for our deceased in all the Masses we participate in. The commemoration of the dead is part of the Eucharistic Prayer; it follows the Mystery of Faith after the consecration, when the priest asks the Lord to remember those who have gone before us, who have "fallen asleep" in the peace of Christ. Be sure to silently include your own deceased family members and friends in this prayer.

Taking part in funeral Masses is also a great act of charity, both for the living family members who are grieving their loss and for the deceased in need of prayer. When possible, it's also good to have Mass celebrated for the deceased on the anniversary of their death.

The Rosary

After the Holy Sacrifice of the Mass, the greatest intercessory prayer we can offer for our dead is the Rosary of the Blessed Virgin Mary. It is a contemplative as well as an intercessory prayer. In the Rosary we ponder the events of the redemption one by one. Each decade's mystery re-presents an event in the life of Christ and the plan of salvation, so that every time we pray the Rosary, we renew our faith in Jesus, in his triumph over sin and death, and our hope in the resurrection of the dead.

As we pray the Rosary, we call upon Mary, Mother of God and mother of all people, the mother of consolation and mercy. We ask her to intercede with her Son for all who are in need. As she never refused God anything, we know that neither will he refuse her any request. Thus, we bring to Mary all our deceased in purgatory, trusting that she will petition God on their behalf.

There are many indulgences attached to praying the Rosary.

Indulgences

Sin has consequences: eternal and temporal (or "temporary") punishment. In the sacrament of Reconciliation, our sins and any eternal punishment connected with them are completely forgiven, but the temporal consequences remain. These consequences are the atonement or reparation that need to be made for those sins. This can be done both through acts of penance and indulgences. An indulgence is the removal of some (a partial indulgence) or all (a plenary indulgence) of the temporal punishment due for sins already forgiven (see CCC 1471–1472). An indulgence can be gained for oneself or applied to the deceased for their purification. An indulgence is a gift received through the application of the sufferings and merits of Jesus our Redeemer, the prayers and good works of the Blessed Virgin Mary, and the prayers and good works of all the saints. This is a treasury of infinite value, one that can never be exhausted (see CCC 1475–1479).

Indulgences are attached to certain prayers and good works, such as participating in the Mass, making a visit to the Blessed Sacrament, praying the Rosary, making the Stations of the Cross, praying the Divine Mercy Chaplet, saying prayers for the dead, giving alms, or carrying out acts of self-denial. There are other indulgenced practices as well.[3] When we pray, it's good to renew our intention to gain indulgences for the souls in purgatory. In doing so, we are helping the deceased pay their debt to God and thus be united with him more quickly.

To gain indulgences it is necessary:

- To be in the state of grace (i.e. free of serious sin and living in friendship with God)
- To have the interior disposition of complete detachment from sin, even venial (minor) sin
- To sacramentally confess one's sins
- To receive the Holy Eucharist
- To pray for the intentions of the pope

It is good, but not necessary, to receive sacramental Confession and especially Holy Communion on the same day as the indulgenced prayer or work. However, if this is not possible, it should be carried out as soon as possible within several days before or after the indulgenced act.[4]

Friendship with the Souls in Purgatory

We began this chapter by considering how we can help our deceased, but the help is not all one way; the souls in purgatory also intercede for us. They are so grateful for our prayers and good works on their behalf that they, in turn, pray for our spiritual and temporal needs. Because they can no longer sin and are so filled with love of God, they are especially loved by him, and their prayers are very powerful before him. Just as I ask earthly friends to pray for me, so I ask my deceased friends and family members to pray for me and for the needs of those I love. Jesus encourages us to do this when he promises that whenever two or three ask for anything in his name, it will be done (see Mt 18:19). What's more, those we have aided and comforted through our prayers for their release from purgatory will continue to intercede for us even afterward when they are in heaven.

So many saints attest to this. Through prayer, our connection with our dearly departed grows stronger and they become our special protectors, helping us to recognize the pitfalls around us and interceding for us with God.

Saint John Paul II encourages us to pray for the souls in purgatory not only for their sake, but also for our own:

> In entrusting them to the Lord, we recognize our solidarity with them and share in their salvation in this wondrous mystery of the communion of saints. . . . I therefore encourage Catholics to pray fervently for the dead, for their family members, and for all our brothers and sisters who have died, that they may obtain the remission of the punishments due to their sins and may hear the Lord's call: "Come, O my dear soul, to eternal repose in the arms of my goodness, which has prepared eternal delights for you".[5]

Keep up your relationship with those who have gone on before you. Do not let that friendship die, for the living and the deceased can be of real help to each other. All who die in God's grace, even while they are still being purified in purgatory, are part of the communion of saints, where a reciprocal communication of spiritual help and goods continues to take place between the members of Christ's Mystical Body in heaven, on earth, and in purgatory (see CCC 962). Make friends with souls in purgatory whom you may not even know, but who have gone through life situations similar to yours. They will know how to inspire you and intercede for you. Are you struggling with someone or anxious about something? Ask those deceased who have been caught up in similar struggles to help you through their prayer of intercession. In turn, help them with your prayers for their speedy purification so that they may enjoy eternal happiness with God more quickly. If we are generous with the deceased, they will be even more generous with us. The following are some prayers addressed to our beloved dead.

Remember Us

Holy suffering souls, who can obtain so many graces for us, remember us amid your sufferings. I will work unceasingly to obtain for you the joys of heaven, and I know you will plead for me.

I beg, both for myself and for my relatives, benefactors, friends, and enemies, pardon of our sins and the grace of perseverance in good, so we may save our souls. Set us free from all misfortunes, miseries, sicknesses, trials, and labors.

Obtain for us peace of heart; assist us in all our actions; help us promptly in all our spiritual and temporal needs; console and defend us in dangers. Pray for the pope, for the Church, for peace between nations, for rulers, and for tranquility among peoples. Grant that we may one day all rejoice together in paradise forever and ever. Amen.

Blessed Mary of Providence

Covenant Prayer

Blessed souls,
you are suffering and asking my intercession;
I am in great danger and need, and I await your
aid and protection.
For this week (*month, or year*)
I will offer all my prayers and especially all my
good works for you.
And you in turn remember my needs;
deliver me from the dangers I face,
and obtain for me this grace; (*mention it*).
And let the first of you to enter heaven not cease
to plead for me

before the divine mercy until I, too, arrive there. May the Sacred Heart bless this agreement.

Amen.

Blessed James Alberione

Prayer of Intercession

Holy souls of purgatory—family members, friends, anyone I was connected to in life, especially N., but even those who remain unknown to me—I pray God in his mercy and compassion to release you soon into the heavenly kingdom of his peace. In my love for you and in gratitude for your prayers for me, I offer my Masses, prayers, and small works of mercy for your relief and liberation.

I ask that you, too, intercede for me for the graces I need to live my life in union with the Father's will, in grateful love for the sacrifice of his only-begotten Son, and in ready obedience to the inspirations of the Spirit. Help me to keep my heart focused on knowing, loving, and serving God in this life, so that I may join you in being happy with God forever in heaven. Amen.

I Promise Never to Forget You

O holy souls, I promise never to forget you and to pray to the Most High for your release. I beseech you to respond to this offering that I make to you. Obtain for us peace of heart; assist us in all our actions; console and defend us in our dangers; that we may one day all rejoice together in paradise.

O God the Creator and Redeemer of all the faithful, grant the souls of your departed servants the remission of their sins, that they may obtain the joys of heaven. We ask this through Christ, our Lord. Amen.

Saint Odilo of Cluny

III

Praying with Scripture for the Departed

> This is my comfort in my distress,
> that your promise gives me life.
>
> —*Psalm 119:50*

When we pray with the word of God, we pray with God himself, for he is the author of Sacred Scripture. His word challenges and consoles and, as the author of Hebrews attests, God's word is living and active. May the psalms and Scripture texts in this chapter enrich your prayer and be a source of consolation as you pray for your deceased family and friends. You may even want to pray these texts, imagining your departed praying the same words with you.

Psalms of Comfort

Psalm 23

The LORD is my shepherd, I shall not want.
He makes me lie down in green pastures;
he leads me beside still waters;
he restores my soul.
He leads me in right paths
for his name's sake.

Even though I walk through the darkest valley,
I fear no evil;
for you are with me;
your rod and your staff—
they comfort me.

You prepare a table before me
in the presence of my enemies;
you anoint my head with oil;
my cup overflows.
Surely goodness and mercy shall follow me
all the days of my life,
and I shall dwell in the house of the LORD
my whole life long.

Psalm 27

The LORD is my light and my salvation;
    whom shall I fear?
The LORD is the stronghold of my life;
    of whom shall I be afraid?

When evildoers assail me
    to devour my flesh—
my adversaries and foes—
    they shall stumble and fall.

Though an army encamp against me,
    my heart shall not fear;
though war rise up against me,
    yet I will be confident.

One thing I asked of the LORD,
    that will I seek after:
to live in the house of the LORD
    all the days of my life,
to behold the beauty of the LORD,
    and to inquire in his temple.

For he will hide me in his shelter
    in the day of trouble;
he will conceal me under the cover of his tent;
    he will set me high on a rock.

Now my head is lifted up
    above my enemies all around me,
and I will offer in his tent
    sacrifices with shouts of joy;
I will sing and make melody to the LORD.

Hear, O LORD, when I cry aloud,
    be gracious to me and answer me!
"Come," my heart says, "seek his face!"
    Your face, LORD, do I seek.
    Do not hide your face from me.

Do not turn your servant away in anger,
    you who have been my help.
Do not cast me off, do not forsake me,
    O God of my salvation!
If my father and mother forsake me,
    the LORD will take me up.

Teach me your way, O LORD,
    and lead me on a level path
    because of my enemies.
Do not give me up to the will of my adversaries,
    for false witnesses have risen against me,
    and they are breathing out violence.

I believe that I shall see the goodness of the LORD
    in the land of the living.

Wait for the LORD;
be strong, and let your heart take courage;
wait for the LORD!

Psalm 42

As a deer longs for flowing streams,
so my soul longs for you, O God.
My soul thirsts for God,
for the living God.
When shall I come and behold
the face of God?
My tears have been my food
day and night,
while people say to me continually,
"Where is your God?"

These things I remember,
as I pour out my soul:
how I went with the throng,
and led them in procession to the house of God,
with glad shouts and songs of thanksgiving,
a multitude keeping festival.
Why are you cast down, O my soul,
and why are you disquieted within me?

Hope in God; for I shall again praise him,
  my help and my God.

My soul is cast down within me;
  therefore I remember you
from the land of Jordan and of Hermon,
  from Mount Mizar.
Deep calls to deep
  at the thunder of your cataracts;
all your waves and your billows
  have gone over me.
By day the LORD commands his steadfast love,
  and at night his song is with me,
  a prayer to the God of my life.

I say to God, my rock,
  "Why have you forgotten me?
Why must I walk about mournfully
  because the enemy oppresses me?"
As with a deadly wound in my body,
  my adversaries taunt me,
while they say to me continually,
  "Where is your God?"

Why are you cast down, O my soul,
  and why are you disquieted within me?
Hope in God; for I shall again praise him,
  my help and my God.

Psalm 63

O God, you are my God, I seek you,
    my soul thirsts for you;
my flesh faints for you,
    as in a dry and weary land where there is
        no water.
So I have looked upon you in the sanctuary,
    beholding your power and glory.
Because your steadfast love is better than life,
    my lips will praise you.
So I will bless you as long as I live;
    I will lift up my hands and call on
        your name.

My soul is satisfied as with a rich feast,
    and my mouth praises you with joyful lips
when I think of you on my bed,
    and meditate on you in the watches of
        the night;
for you have been my help,
    and in the shadow of your wings I sing
        for joy.
My soul clings to you;
    your right hand upholds me.

But those who seek to destroy my life

shall go down into the depths of the earth;
they shall be given over to the power of the sword,
they shall be prey for jackals.
But the king shall rejoice in God;
all who swear by him shall exult,
for the mouths of liars will be stopped.

Psalm 103

Bless the LORD, O my soul,
and all that is within me,
bless his holy name.
Bless the LORD, O my soul,
and do not forget all his benefits—
who forgives all your iniquity,
who heals all your diseases,
who redeems your life from the Pit,
who crowns you with steadfast love and mercy,
who satisfies you with good as long as you live
so that your youth is renewed like the eagle's.

The LORD works vindication
and justice for all who are oppressed.
He made known his ways to Moses,

his acts to the people of Israel.
The LORD is merciful and gracious,
slow to anger and abounding in steadfast
love.
He will not always accuse,
nor will he keep his anger forever.
He does not deal with us according to our sins,
nor repay us according to our iniquities.
For as the heavens are high above the earth,
so great is his steadfast love toward those
who fear him;
as far as the east is from the west,
so far he removes our transgressions from us.
As a father has compassion for his children,
so the LORD has compassion for those who
fear him.
For he knows how we were made;
he remembers that we are dust.

As for mortals, their days are like grass;
they flourish like a flower of the field;
for the wind passes over it, and it is gone,
and its place knows it no more.
But the steadfast love of the LORD is from everlasting to everlasting
on those who fear him,

and his righteousness to children's children,
to those who keep his covenant
and remember to do his commandments.

The LORD has established his throne in the heavens,
and his kingdom rules over all.
Bless the LORD, O you his angels,
you mighty ones who do his bidding,
obedient to his spoken word.
Bless the LORD, all his hosts,
his ministers that do his will.
Bless the LORD, all his works,
in all places of his dominion.
Bless the LORD, O my soul.

Penitential Psalms

These are traditionally prayed for the dead.

Psalm 6

(First penitential psalm)

O Lord, do not rebuke me in your anger,
    or discipline me in your wrath.
Be gracious to me, O Lord, for I am languishing;
    O Lord, heal me, for my bones are shaking
    with terror.
My soul also is struck with terror,
    while you, O Lord —how long?

Turn, O Lord, save my life;
    deliver me for the sake of your steadfast love.
For in death there is no remembrance of you;
    in Sheol who can give you praise?

I am weary with my moaning;
    every night I flood my bed with tears;
    I drench my couch with my weeping.
My eyes waste away because of grief;
    they grow weak because of all my foes.

Depart from me, all you workers of evil,
for the Lord has heard the sound of my weeping.
The Lord has heard my supplication;
the Lord accepts my prayer.
All my enemies shall be ashamed and struck with terror;
they shall turn back, and in a moment be put to shame.

Psalm 32

(Second penitential psalm)

Happy are those whose transgression is forgiven,
whose sin is covered.
Happy are those to whom the Lord imputes no iniquity,
and in whose spirit there is no deceit.

While I kept silence, my body wasted away
through my groaning all day long.
For day and night your hand was heavy upon me;
my strength was dried up as by the heat of summer.

Then I acknowledged my sin to you,
and I did not hide my iniquity;

I said, "I will confess my transgressions to the
    LORD,"
        and you forgave the guilt of my sin.

Therefore let all who are faithful
        offer prayer to you;
at a time of distress, the rush of mighty waters
        shall not reach them.
You are a hiding place for me;
        you preserve me from trouble;
        you surround me with glad cries of
            deliverance.

I will instruct you and teach you the way you
    should go;
        I will counsel you with my eye upon you.
Do not be like a horse or a mule, without under-
    standing,
        whose temper must be curbed with bit and
            bridle,
        else it will not stay near you.

Many are the torments of the wicked,
        but steadfast love surrounds those who
            trust in the LORD.
Be glad in the LORD and rejoice, O righteous,
        and shout for joy, all you upright in heart.

Psalm 38

(Third penitential psalm)

O LORD, do not rebuke me in your anger,
	or discipline me in your wrath.
For your arrows have sunk into me,
	and your hand has come down on me.

There is no soundness in my flesh
	because of your indignation;
there is no health in my bones
	because of my sin.
For my iniquities have gone over my head;
	they weigh like a burden too heavy for me.

My wounds grow foul and fester
	because of my foolishness;
I am utterly bowed down and prostrate;
	all day long I go around mourning.
For my loins are filled with burning,
	and there is no soundness in my flesh.
I am utterly spent and crushed;
	I groan because of the tumult of my heart.

O Lord, all my longing is known to you;
	my sighing is not hidden from you.

My heart throbs, my strength fails me;
as for the light of my eyes—it also has gone from me.
My friends and companions stand aloof from my affliction,
and my neighbors stand far off.

Those who seek my life lay their snares;
those who seek to hurt me speak of ruin,
and meditate treachery all day long.

But I am like the deaf, I do not hear;
like the mute, who cannot speak.
Truly, I am like one who does not hear,
and in whose mouth is no retort.

But it is for you, O Lord, that I wait;
it is you, O Lord my God, who will answer.
For I pray, "Only do not let them rejoice over me,
those who boast against me when my foot slips."

For I am ready to fall,
and my pain is ever with me.
I confess my iniquity;
I am sorry for my sin.
Those who are my foes without cause are mighty,

and many are those who hate me
wrongfully.
Those who render me evil for good
are my adversaries because I follow after
good.

Do not forsake me, O Lord;
O my God, do not be far from me;
make haste to help me,
O Lord, my salvation.

Psalm 51

(Fourth penitential psalm)

Have mercy on me, O God,
according to your steadfast love;
according to your abundant mercy
blot out my transgressions.
Wash me thoroughly from my iniquity,
and cleanse me from my sin.

For I know my transgressions,
and my sin is ever before me.
Against you, you alone, have I sinned,
and done what is evil in your sight,
so that you are justified in your sentence

and blameless when you pass judgment.
Indeed, I was born guilty,
a sinner when my mother conceived me.

You desire truth in the inward being;
therefore teach me wisdom in my secret heart.
Purge me with hyssop, and I shall be clean;
wash me, and I shall be whiter than snow.
Let me hear joy and gladness;
let the bones that you have crushed rejoice.
Hide your face from my sins,
and blot out all my iniquities.

Create in me a clean heart, O God,
and put a new and right spirit within me.
Do not cast me away from your presence,
and do not take your holy spirit from me.
Restore to me the joy of your salvation,
and sustain in me a willing spirit.

Then I will teach transgressors your ways,
and sinners will return to you.
Deliver me from bloodshed, O God,
O God of my salvation,
and my tongue will sing aloud of your deliverance.

O Lord, open my lips,
and my mouth will declare your praise.
For you have no delight in sacrifice;
if I were to give a burnt-offering, you would not be pleased.
The sacrifice acceptable to God is a broken spirit;
a broken and contrite heart, O God, you will not despise.

Do good to Zion in your good pleasure;
rebuild the walls of Jerusalem,
then you will delight in right sacrifices,
in burnt offerings and whole burnt offerings;
then bulls will be offered on your altar.

Psalm 102

(Fifth penitential psalm)

Hear my prayer, O LORD;
let my cry come to you.
Do not hide your face from me
in the day of my distress.
Incline your ear to me;
answer me speedily in the day when I call.

For my days pass away like smoke,
    and my bones burn like a furnace.
My heart is stricken and withered like grass;
    I am too wasted to eat my bread.
Because of my loud groaning
    my bones cling to my skin.
I am like an owl of the wilderness,
    like a little owl of the waste places.
I lie awake;
    I am like a lonely bird on the housetop.
All day long my enemies taunt me;
    those who deride me use my name for a
        curse.
For I eat ashes like bread,
    and mingle tears with my drink,
because of your indignation and anger;
    for you have lifted me up and thrown me
        aside.
My days are like an evening shadow;
    I wither away like grass.

But you, O LORD, are enthroned forever;
    your name endures to all generations.
You will rise up and have compassion on Zion,
    for it is time to favor it;
    the appointed time has come.

For your servants hold its stones dear,
and have pity on its dust.
The nations will fear the name of the LORD,
and all the kings of the earth your glory.
For the LORD will build up Zion;
he will appear in his glory.
He will regard the prayer of the destitute,
and will not despise their prayer.

Let this be recorded for a generation to come,
so that a people yet unborn may praise the LORD:
that he looked down from his holy height,
from heaven the LORD looked at the earth,
to hear the groans of the prisoners,
to set free those who were doomed to die;
so that the name of the LORD may be declared in Zion,
and his praise in Jerusalem,
when peoples gather together,
and kingdoms, to worship the LORD.

He has broken my strength in midcourse;
he has shortened my days.
"O my God," I say, "do not take me away
at the mid-point of my life,

you whose years endure
throughout all generations."

Long ago you laid the foundation of the earth,
and the heavens are the work of your hands.
They will perish, but you endure;
they will all wear out like a garment.
You change them like clothing, and they pass away;
but you are the same, and your years have no end.
The children of your servants shall live secure;
their offspring shall be established in your presence.

Psalm 130

(Sixth penitential psalm)

Out of the depths I cry to you, O LORD.
Lord, hear my voice!
Let your ears be attentive
to the voice of my supplications!

If you, O LORD, should mark iniquities,
Lord, who could stand?
But there is forgiveness with you,
so that you may be revered.

I wait for the LORD, my soul waits,
and in his word I hope;
my soul waits for the Lord
more than those who watch for the morning,
more than those who watch for the morning.

O Israel, hope in the LORD!
For with the LORD there is steadfast love,
and with him is great power to redeem.
It is he who will redeem Israel
from all its iniquities.

Psalm 143

(Seventh penitential psalm)

Hear my prayer, O LORD;
give ear to my supplications in your faithfulness;
answer me in your righteousness.
Do not enter into judgment with your servant,
for no one living is righteous before you.

For the enemy has pursued me,
crushing my life to the ground,
making me sit in darkness like those long dead.
Therefore my spirit faints within me;
my heart within me is appalled.

I remember the days of old,
    I think about all your deeds,
    I meditate on the works of your hands.
I stretch out my hands to you;
    my soul thirsts for you like a parched land.

Answer me quickly, O LORD;
    my spirit fails.
Do not hide your face from me,
    or I shall be like those who go down to the
        Pit.
Let me hear of your steadfast love in the morning,
    for in you I put my trust.
Teach me the way I should go,
    for to you I lift up my soul.

Save me, O LORD, from my enemies;
    I have fled to you for refuge.
Teach me to do your will,
    for you are my God.
Let your good spirit lead me
    on a level path.

For your name's sake, O LORD, preserve my life.
    In your righteousness bring me out of trouble.
In your steadfast love cut off my enemies,
    and destroy all my adversaries,
    for I am your servant.

Scripture Texts for Meditation

Some of the most beautiful and consoling Scripture texts are those that speak about the promise of eternal life with God when this earthly pilgrimage is finished. May these passages not only strengthen our faith in the resurrection of the dead, but also fortify our hope and deepen our bond with those who have gone before us.

The Destiny of the Righteous (Wisdom 3:1–9)
Jesus Will Raise Us Up (John 6:37–40)
Jesus the Resurrection and the Life (John 11:17–27)
Jesus the Way to the Father (John 14:1–6)
God's Love in Christ Jesus (Romans 8:31b–39)
The Resurrected Body (1 Corinthians 15:50b–57)
Living by Faith (2 Corinthians 5:1–7)

IV

Prayers for Our Own Beloved Dead

Everything that the Father gives me will come to me, and anyone who comes to me I will never drive away.

—*John 6:37*

What if we are unsure whether a family member or friend died in God's grace? For example, maybe he or she was not raised in any faith or fell away from the practice of it, had problems living according to the teaching of Jesus and his Church, or led a life marked by some form of addiction. We need to always remember that only God knows the struggle and the heart of each person. Our loved ones' actions may not have been a rejection of God, but rather a result of woundedness, weakness, or lack of knowledge. And in a last moment unperceived by us, they may have silently reached out to God for help, asking for mercy. God rejects no one who turns to him, as the dying thief on Calvary witnesses (see Lk 23:43). Thus, it is always important to pray for our dead. Divine mercy desires to liberate all these souls and open to them the gates of heaven as soon as possible—asking our collaboration through prayers and good works. May our love for the deceased compel us to pray for them with Jesus Christ, through Jesus Christ, and in Jesus Christ.

Prayer for a Deceased Loved One

Lord Jesus, with hope and confidence I entrust to you the soul of N., whose loss I feel so deeply. You know and understand my grief, for you yourself felt the loss of your foster father, Joseph, with whom you shared most of your life, and of Lazarus, who was such a good friend and support to you in your ministry. Be my strength and consolation in my own great sorrow.

Accept my pain and prayers as an offering for the soul of N. Have mercy on him/her for any residue of sin that remains to be cleansed. Purify him/her in your most precious Blood and take him/her to heaven as soon as possible to enjoy the eternal happiness of your presence and that of your Father and the Holy Spirit. I find peace in the thought that N. and I will meet again someday to live eternally in that dwelling you have prepared for us. Amen.

Let Me Never Forget

O God of those who are silently summoning me to enter into your life, never let me forget my dead, my living. May my love and faithfulness to them be a pledge of my belief in you, the God of eternal life.

Let me not be deaf to the call of their silence, which is the surest and sincerest word of their love. May this word of theirs continue to accompany me, even after they have taken leave of me to enter into you, for thus their love comes all the closer to me. O my soul, never forget your dead, for they live. And the life they live, now unveiled in eternal light, is your own life, which will one day be revealed also in you. . . .

My waning life is becoming more and more a life with the dead. I live more and more with those who have gone before me into the dark night where no one can work. By your life-giving grace, O Lord, let it become ever more a life of faith in your light, shining now dimly in this earthly night. Let me live with the living who have preceded me in the sign of faith, who have gone before me into the bright day of eternal life, when no one need work, because you yourself are this day, the fullness of all reality, the God of the living.

When I pray, "Grant them eternal rest, O Lord, and let your perpetual light shine upon them," let my words be only the echo of the prayer of love that they themselves are speaking for me in the silence of eternity.

O my soul, never forget the dead. O God of all the living, do not forget me, the dead one, but come one day to be my life, as you are theirs. Amen.[6]

Karl Rahner, SJ

Prayer for Deceased Parents

Heavenly Father, you have called my mother/father to yourself. I still miss her/him but want her/him to receive the joy of everlasting life with you. You entrusted your own beloved Son to the care of an earthly mother and father and commanded us to always honor and love our parents. I thank you that my parents brought me into this world, and I trust that you will reward them for every sacrifice they made and for every good deed. In your mercy, have pity on the soul of my mother/father and forgive her/his sins. Bring her/him soon to live with you in the joy of your love. May I join my parents in your heavenly kingdom at the end of my own earthly life to praise and bless you forever. Amen.

For a Deceased Spouse

Jesus, my Savior, hear my prayer as I grieve the loss of my spouse. I feel so alone now. Help me to surrender to your divine will. I know that you love my spouse, who, I pray, is already rejoicing in your presence or will be soon. Accept my loss and the pain of separation as an offering of intercession for his/her soul. Let us never become disconnected but remain always united in prayer. Through the merits of your most holy passion and death, cleanse him/her of all imperfection and stain of sin so that he/she may be admitted to heaven as quickly as possible. May I one day be reunited with my spouse in heaven, where we both can praise you for all eternity. Amen.

Parent's Prayer at the Loss of a Child

Loving Father, the pain of losing a child must be one of the worst sufferings on earth! You know my pain and my grief. Receive my daughter/son into your arms and heart to be forever with you in paradise where there is no sorrow, weeping, or pain, but only the fullness of peace and joy. If my child came to you with any stain of sin on her/his soul, purify these as quickly as possible through the merits of your own dearly beloved Son. Do not let my child be separated from you, and, once she/he is in your embrace, hold and caress her/him for me. When I leave this world may my daughter/son greet and welcome me into eternal life. Amen.

For a Departed Sibling

Lord God, you have called my sibling home. I realize that we are all destined for eternal life with you, and that lightens my grieving and gives me hope. I thank you for the special times I had with N., and I ask pardon for the times that I did not appreciate the gift. Jesus, through the merits of your passion and death, forgive the sins of N. and relieve the sufferings of purgatory. Reward the good my sibling did on this earth and the love we shared. Receive the soul of my brother/sister into your own wonderful light, and may we one day both be united with you in eternal joy. Amen.

For a Deceased Friend

Merciful Father, I commend my dear friend N. into your loving embrace. Thank you for the precious gift of friendship and for the memories that I will always cherish. Just as Jesus raised his friend Lazarus from the dead, so raise my friend up, forgive his/her sins and shortcomings through the merits of your beloved Son, and receive him/her into your joy. May he/she rest in peace. Amen.

For a Deceased Priest

O God, you called your servant, N., to the sacred ministry of Jesus Christ as his priest, giving him the sublime power to offer the Holy Sacrifice of the Mass, to bring the Body and Blood of your Son Jesus Christ down upon the altar, and to absolve sins in your holy name. Reward his faithfulness and forgive his faults, admitting him speedily into your holy presence, so that he may enjoy the recompense of his labors forever.

Dear Father, I pray also for those deceased priests who have heard my confessions and given me the absolution of my sins, and who have provided me with spiritual direction, encouragement, and comfort. Welcome to the wedding feast of the Lamb of God all those priests who fed me with the precious Body and Blood of Jesus, your Son. May all those who broke the bread of the Word and instructed me in the faith be rewarded a hundredfold in eternity. I ask this through Jesus Christ, your Son, our Lord. Amen.

Prayer After an Unexpected Death

Jesus, I feel so shaken by the unexpected death of N. I know that you did not leave him/her alone in his/her final moment, but that you were there with your mercy and consolation. Please help me accept the suddenness of my loss, abandon myself to your divine will, and trust in your loving compassion. I want to think that N. is already with you in heaven, but I know how subject we are to sin and temptation. I pray you to purify N. through the merits of your blood poured out for us on Calvary and applied in every Mass. Accept my prayers united to yours and admit N. soon into the dwelling you have prepared for him/her. Amen.

Prayer After a Violent Death

Lord Jesus, our Savior and Redeemer, how troubled I am by the violent death of N. I can make no sense of it. Teach me to pray with you, "Father, forgive them. . . ." I need your help and your grace to do that. Help me to forgive even in the name of and for the sake of N. I pray that in that dark and senseless moment, you were there to receive him/her in your infinite mercy and that the suffering of N. was united to your own passion and death for the purification of his/her soul. May he/she soon rejoice with you in paradise where there is no more weeping and no more pain. I ask this in your name and through your merits. Amen.

Prayer in Time of Suicide

Lord Jesus Christ, I have no place else to go but to kneel at the foot of the Cross. The death of someone so dear to me in this awful way leaves me completely confused and disoriented. It is so bitter. I am haunted by the thought that I could have done something, that I might have prevented this terrible disaster. But I don't know. I must entrust my dear one to you. There is no place else to turn. My dear one, now taken from me by the weakness of the human mind, by the inability to cope with the difficulties of life, by the wounds of mental illness, I place in your hands. I trust completely in you that I will see those who have died this way again. I trust that, by your precious Blood and divine mercy in the last moments of life, you receive them, understanding that they have been defeated by life; and that in no way did they mean to go against your will and your law. Help us, O Lord, in this darkness to find you and to believe in your Cross. Amen.[7]

Benedict Groeschel, CFR

For Those Who Gave Their Lives for Others

Lord God, I am so grateful and pray for all, especially family members and friends, who have sacrificed their lives so that we may live in freedom and peace, free from injustice and destruction. I am reminded of the words of your Son, Jesus, "No one has greater love than this, to lay down one's life for one's friends" (Jn 15:13). May I never forget their sacrifice, but always cherish their gift and honor their memory. Welcome these departed heroes into the heavenly home you have prepared for them and bless them forever with your peace and joy. Amen.

Forty Day Prayer

Forty days is an important length of time in Judeo-Christian spirituality, symbolizing purification and/or preparation for a momentous event. Our Lord himself fasted forty days and nights in the desert to prepare himself for his public ministry. In this tradition some cultures offer prayers for their deceased loved ones for forty consecutive days for their entrance into their heavenly reward.

Loving God, I humbly pray you to receive the soul of N., our dearest beloved who has died. Reward the good deeds and the acts of kindness and love that N. performed in life. Forgive all his/her sins, weaknesses, and omissions through the merits of the passion and death of your only-begotten Son. Open the gates of heaven to him/her, Father, welcoming your child who has finally come home to rest in your eternal light and love. May your angels receive this faithful servant, and may he/she continue to assist and watch over us on our pilgrimage through life until we can all be reunited with you. Amen.

V

Traditional Prayers for the Souls in Purgatory

Although he causes grief, he will have compassion according to the abundance of his steadfast love.

—*Lamentations 3:32*

Jesus sacrificed his life so that we might be redeemed, offering every drop of his precious Blood for our salvation. This is part of the infinite treasure of grace won for us by the passion and resurrection of Jesus Christ. Those in purgatory understand this well; they know that they are saved, and they are profoundly grateful to Jesus for this grace, but they also long for the day when they will be freed from their suffering and be united with the Lord. It is a spiritual work of mercy and a great act of charity to pray for the dead, especially for those who are most forgotten. The souls in purgatory rely very much on our prayers to alleviate and shorten their time of purification. God has created us all interdependent precisely for the purpose of helping one another, and the greatest help we can give is prayer.

Eternal Rest Prayer

Eternal rest grant unto them, O Lord, and let perpetual light shine upon them. May they rest in peace. Amen.

May their souls and the souls of all the faithful departed, through the mercy of God, rest in peace. Amen.

Prayer of Saint Gertrude

Eternal Father, I offer you the most precious
Blood of your divine Son, Jesus,
in union with the Masses said throughout the
world today,
for all the holy souls in purgatory, for sinners
everywhere,
for sinners in the universal Church,
those in my own home, and within my family.
Amen.

Heroic Act of Love

My God, for your greater glory, in union with the merits of Jesus and Mary, I offer and surrender the atoning value of all the good I will do and all the prayers I will receive after my death for the holy souls in purgatory. Dispose of everything according to your divine will.

Attributed to Saint Gertrude

Morning Offering for the Souls in Purgatory

Divine Heart of Jesus, I offer you every thought, desire, word, and deed this day as a loving petition to your mercy on behalf of the suffering souls in purgatory, especially for those who have no one to pray for them. I unite all the difficulties, sufferings, and contradictions of this day to your most sacred passion and in union with Jesus in the Blessed Sacrament. Drawing upon your merits and trusting in your grace, I promise to bear everything with patience so that these souls may be speedily released from their place of purification to see, love, and enjoy you for all eternity. Amen.

For the Faithful Departed

My Jesus, by your sufferings and during your agony in the garden, your scourging and crowning with thorns, your journey to Calvary, and your crucifixion and death, have mercy on the souls of the faithful departed, especially on those who have no one to pray for them. Deliver them from their suffering and admit them to your tender embrace in heaven.

Our Father, Hail Mary, Eternal Rest.

O God, Creator and Redeemer of all people, grant to all departed souls the remission of their sins. With heartfelt prayer I ask that you grant them the pardon for their sins that they so greatly desire.

Our Father, Hail Mary, Eternal Rest.

May my prayer, Lord, help the souls of the faithful departed, that you may free them from their sins and make them sharers in your redemption.

Our Father, Hail Mary, Eternal Rest.

Second-Century Prayer for the Dead

Through your goodness, O Lord, receive in tranquility and peace the souls of your servants who have departed the present life to come to you. Grant them rest and place them in the habitations of light, the abodes of blessed spirits. Give them the life that will not age, good things that will not pass away, and delights that have no end, through Jesus Christ, our Lord. Amen.

Attributed to Saint Ignatius of Antioch

The Seven Days Prayer for the Dead

Sunday

O Lord God almighty, I beseech you, by the Precious Blood that your divine Son Jesus shed in the Garden of Gethsemane, deliver the souls in purgatory, especially the one most forsaken and forgotten; and bring them into your glory, there to praise and bless you forever. Amen.

Our Father, Hail Mary, Eternal Rest.

Monday

O Lord God almighty, I beseech you, by the Precious Blood that your divine Son Jesus shed in his cruel scourging, deliver the souls in purgatory, and especially the one nearest to its entrance into your glory, that it may soon begin to praise and bless you forever. Amen.

Our Father, Hail Mary, Eternal Rest.

Tuesday

O Lord God almighty, I beseech you, by the Precious Blood that your divine Son Jesus shed in his bitter crowning with thorns, deliver the souls in purgatory, and among them all especially the one in most need of our prayers, that it may not long be delayed before it comes to praise you in your glory and bless you forever. Amen.

Our Father, Hail Mary, Eternal Rest.

Wednesday

O Lord God almighty, I beseech you, by the Precious Blood that your divine Son Jesus shed on the streets of Jerusalem when he carried the Cross upon his sacred shoulders, deliver the souls in purgatory, and especially the one richest in merits in your sight, that having soon attained the glory that awaits it, it may praise and bless you forever. Amen.

Our Father, Hail Mary, Eternal Rest.

Thursday

O Lord God almighty, I beseech you, by the Precious Body and Blood of your divine Son Jesus, which he himself on the night before his passion gave as food and drink to his beloved apostles and left to his whole Church to be a perpetual sacrifice and the life-giving nourishment of his faithful people, deliver the souls in purgatory, and especially the one that was most devoted to this mystery of infinite love, that it may praise you together with your divine Son and the Holy Spirit in your glory forever. Amen.

Our Father, Hail Mary, Eternal Rest.

Friday

O Lord God almighty, I beseech you, by the Precious Blood that your divine Son shed on this day upon the tree of the Cross, especially from his most sacred hands and feet, deliver the souls in purgatory, and especially the one for whom I am most bound to pray, that no neglect of mine may hinder it from praising you in your glory and blessing you forever. Amen.

Our Father, Hail Mary, Eternal Rest.

Saturday

O Lord God almighty, I beseech you, by the Precious Blood that gushed forth from the side of your divine Son Jesus in the presence of and to the great sorrow of his most holy Mother, deliver the souls in purgatory, and especially the one most devoted to this noble lady, that it may enter quickly into your glory, there to praise you in her and her in you, through all eternity. Amen.

Our Father, Hail Mary, Eternal Rest.

Attributed to Saint Nicholas of Tolentino

Offering of Christ's Passion

Look down, O Father of compassion, from your holy throne upon the souls detained in purgatory. Look upon all the pains and sufferings wherewith they are being purified; regard now the cries and tears that they pour out to you. Hear the prayers and supplications wherewith they entreat your mercy and be merciful to them. Remember, O most compassionate Father, all the sufferings which your Son endured for them; remember his precious Blood shed in such abundance for them. Call to mind the most bitter death that he suffered for them and have mercy on them. For all the sins they have ever committed against you, I offer you the most holy life and words of your most beloved Son; for all their negligence, I offer you his most fervent desires toward you; for all their omissions, I offer you the great abundance of his merits; for their every insult and wrong to you, I offer you the sweet submission with which he honored you. Finally, for all the chastisements that they have ever incurred, I offer you all the mortifications, fasting, watching, the labors and afflictions, wounds and stripes, passion and death, which he endured in such spotless innocence and with such loving eagerness, beseeching you now to let your justice be satisfied toward them, and to lead them forth into everlasting joy. Amen.

Saint Gertrude

Offering of the Five Wounds of Jesus

1. We offer to you, Eternal Father, Father of mercies, for those souls so dear to you that are now in purgatory, the most precious Blood that flowed from the wound in the left foot of Jesus, your Son, our Savior, and the grief of Mary, his most loving Mother, present on Calvary when he was so cruelly wounded.

Our Father, Hail Mary, Eternal Rest.

2. We offer to you, Eternal Father, Father of mercies, for those souls so dear to you that are now in purgatory, the most precious Blood that flowed from the wound in the right foot of Jesus, your Son, our Savior, and the grief of Mary, his most loving Mother, present on Calvary when he was so cruelly wounded.

Our Father, Hail Mary, Eternal Rest.

3. We offer to you, Eternal Father, Father of mercies, for those souls so dear to you that are now in purgatory, the most precious Blood that flowed from the wound in the left hand of Jesus, your Son, our Savior, and the grief of Mary, his dearest Mother, present on Calvary when he was so cruelly wounded.

Our Father, Hail Mary, Eternal Rest.

4. We offer to you, Eternal Father, Father of mercies, for those souls so dear to you that are now in purgatory, the most precious Blood that flowed from the wound in the right hand of Jesus, your Son, our Savior, and the grief of Mary, his dearest Mother, present on Calvary when he was so cruelly wounded.

Our Father, Hail Mary, Eternal Rest.

5. We offer to you, Eternal Father, Father of mercies, for those souls so dear to you that are now in purgatory, the most precious Blood and the water that flowed from the opened side of Jesus, your Son, our Savior, and the grief of Mary, his most loving Mother, present on Calvary when he was so cruelly wounded.

Our Father, Hail Mary, Eternal Rest.

And now, in order that our poor prayers may be made more worthy to be offered to God, we turn to you, most gracious Lord Jesus, and entreat you to offer to the Eternal Father the sacred wounds in your feet and hands and sacred side, together with your most precious Blood, agony, and death. And you, too, most sorrowful Mother, Mary, offer up, with the bitter passion of your most beloved Son, the sighs and tears and all your grief in his sufferings; in order that, through the merits of them all, the souls now suffering in the burning flames of purgatory may obtain relief and refreshment, and thus, freed from that place of suffering, they may be clothed with glory in heaven, and there praise the divine mercy forever. Amen.

Byzantine Prayer for the Deceased

O God of all spiritual and corporeal beings,
you trampled death, broke the power of Satan,
and granted life to the whole world.

Now, O Lord, grant also rest to the souls of your departed servants
in a place of light, freshness, and peace, where there is no pain, sorrow, or mourning.

As a gracious God, and loving humankind,
forgive them every transgression committed in word, deed, or thought,
since there is no one alive who has not sinned.
You alone are without sin and your justice is everlasting justice,
and your word is always the truth.

For you are the resurrection, the life, and the
repose of your departed servants,
O Christ our God, and we render glory to you,
together with your Eternal Father, and your
most holy, gracious, and life-giving Spirit,
now and always and for ever and ever. Amen.

Attributed to Saint John Chrysostom

Maronite Prayer for the Departed

O Christ our God, have mercy on the faithful departed, who were clothed in you at Baptism and received your Body and Blood as nourishment and blessing on the path to eternity. May they be worthy to meet you with radiant faces and share in your eternal banquet. May they rest in your heavenly Jerusalem, the city of saints, in the dwellings of light and joy. Amen.

A Syriac Prayer for the Dead

Lord, listen to our voices, hear the prayers we
praise,
and open wide your gates above, we ask of you.
Grant rest to our departed ones who died in hope,

our parents, loved ones, and the teachers of true faith.

Blot out their sins and failings from your books, O Lord,
and bring them safely to your paradise on high.
For those who asked us to remember them in prayer,
forgive their sins and faults committed in your sight.

The dead who have departed from this world in faith
were nourished by your living Body and your Blood.
We pray that they may stand with those at your right hand,
with your apostles Peter and beloved John.

And when all nations stand before your mighty throne,
we ask you not to judge us on our sins and faults.
We raise our voices to adore the Trinity,
the Father, Son, and Holy Spirit, one true God. Amen.

Litany for the Faithful Departed

Lord, have mercy on us. *Christ, have mercy on us.*

Lord, have mercy on us. Christ, hear us.
Christ, graciously hear us.

God the Father of heaven,

Response: *have mercy on the souls of the faithful departed.*

God the Son, Redeemer of the world, ℟.

God the Holy Spirit, ℟.

Holy Trinity, One God, ℟.

Holy Mary,

Response: *pray for the souls of the faithful departed.*

Holy Mother of God, ℟.

Saint Michael, ℟.

Saint Gabriel, ℟.

All you holy angels and archangels, ℟.

Saint John the Baptist, ℟.

Saint Joseph, ℟.

All you holy patriarchs and prophets, ℟.

Saint Peter, ℟.

Saint Paul, ℟.

Saint John, ℟.

All you holy apostles and evangelists, ℟.

Saint Stephen, ℟.

Saint Lawrence, ℟.

All you holy martyrs, ℟.

Saint Gregory, ℟.

Saint Ambrose, ℟.

All you holy bishops and confessors, ℟.

Saint Mary Magdalene, ℟.

Saint Catherine, ℟.

All you holy virgins and widows, ℟.

All you saints of God, ℟.

Be merciful, *pardon them, O Lord.*

Be merciful, *hear us, O Lord.*

From all evil,

Response: *O Lord, deliver them.*

From your wrath, ℟.

From the flame of fire, ℟.

From the region of the shadow of death, ℟.

Through your holy Incarnation, ℟.

Through your Nativity, ℟.

Through your most holy name, ℟.

Through your Baptism and fasting, ℟.

Through the multitude of your tender mercies, ℟.
Through your most bitter passion, ℟.
Through your most sacred wounds, ℟.
Through your most precious Blood, ℟.
Through your ignominious death, by which you destroyed our death, ℟.
Through your glorious Resurrection, ℟.
Through your Ascension, ℟.
Through the outpouring of your Holy Spirit, ℟.
We sinners,

Response: *we beseech you, hear us.*

You who absolved the sinful woman and heard the prayer of the good thief, ℟.
That you release our deceased parents, relations, and benefactors from the bonds of sin, ℟.
That it may please you to have mercy on all who have none to remember or pray for them, ℟.
That it may please you to hasten the day of releasing the faithful detained in purgatory and bring them to eternal peace, ℟.
That it may please you to admit them among your saints, ℟.

Lamb of God, who takes away the sins of the world,
grant them eternal rest.
Lamb of God, who takes away the sins of the world,
grant them eternal rest.
Lamb of God, who takes away the sins of the world,
grant them eternal rest.
Christ, hear us. *Christ, graciously hear us.*

Our Father . . .

Let us pray.

O God, Creator and Redeemer of all the faithful, grant to the souls of your departed servants the remission of all their sins, that through our prayerful supplications they may obtain the pardon which they have always desired. Through Jesus Christ, our Lord.

Litany for the Souls in Purgatory

O Jesus, you suffered and died that all humankind might be saved and brought to eternal happiness. Hear our pleas for mercy on the souls of:

My dear parents, grandparents, and ancestors,

Response: *Jesus, have mercy!*

My brothers and sisters and other near relatives, ℟.

My godparents and Confirmation sponsor, ℟.

My spiritual and temporal benefactors, ℟.

My friends and neighbors, ℟.

My employers and associates, ℟.

Those who inspired and encouraged me by their good example, ℟.

All for whom love or duty calls me to pray, ℟.

Those who have suffered disadvantage or harm because of me, ℟.

Those who have offended me, ℟.

Those who are especially beloved by you, ℟.

Those whose release is near at hand, ℟.

Those who desired most to be united to you, ℟.

Those who tried to be attentive in doing your will, ℟.

Those who now endure the greatest sufferings, ℟.

Those whose release is most remote, ℟.

Those who are least remembered, ℟.

Those who are most deserving because of their services to the Church, ℟.

Those who were kind and good to their neighbor, ℟.

Those who promoted peace, ℟.

Those who promoted life and the rights of the most vulnerable, ℟.

Those who were once rich, ℟.

Those who were once mighty, ℟.

Those who were once spiritually blind, but now see their folly, ℟.

Those who were frivolous, spending their time in idleness, ℟.

Those who misused the media, ℟.

Those poor who did not seek the treasures of heaven, ℟.

Those who devoted little time to prayer, ℟.

Those who were spiritually lazy in performing good works, ℟.

Those who were negligent in receiving the sacraments, ℟.

Habitual sinners, who owe their salvation to a miracle of grace, ℟.

Parents who failed to watch over their children, ℟.

Superiors who were not solicitous for the salvation of those entrusted to them, ℟.

Employers who were unjust toward their employees, ℟.

Those worldly minded, who failed to use their wealth and talent for the service of God, ℟.

Those who witnessed the death of others, but would not think of their own, ℟.

Those who did not provide for their eternal destiny, ℟.

Those whose judgment is more severe because of the many gifts entrusted to them, ℟.

Popes, kings, and world leaders, ℟.

Bishops and their advisors, ℟.

Priests, deacons, seminarians, and members of consecrated life, ℟.

Missionaries, evangelizers, catechists, teachers, and defenders of the faith, ℟.

My own teachers, mentors, and spiritual directors, ℟.

Those who worked generously for the common good, ℟.

Those who promoted what is good and true through the media, ℟.

Those who died on the battlefield, defending our freedoms, ℟.

Those who were buried in the sea, ℟.

Those who served their country and all first responders, ℟.

Those who died of a stroke, a heart attack, or suddenly, ℟.

Those who suffered and died of terminal illnesses, ℟.

Those who died from drug abuse, ℟.

Those who in a moment of darkness took their own life, ℟.

Those who died through an act of violence, ℟.

Those who died in accidents, ℟.

Those who died without the last sacraments of the Church, ℟.

Those who shall die within the next twenty-four hours, ℟.

My own poor soul when I shall appear before your judgment seat, ℟.

Let us pray:

Be mindful, O Lord, of those who have gone before us in the sign of faith. To these, and to all that rest in Christ, grant, we pray, a place of refreshment, light, and peace. Through the same Christ, our Lord. Amen.

Eternal rest.

The Lord's Prayer for the Departed

Our Father who art in heaven. I beg you, O loving Father, to pardon the souls in purgatory for having shut their hearts to you and for failing to worship you as you desire. To atone for their faults, I offer you the love and honor your beloved Son gave you while on earth and the plentiful redemption he won for us, paying the debt of all our sins.

Hallowed be thy name. I beg you, O loving Father, to pardon the souls in purgatory for not having worthily honored your holy name, having seldom invoked it with devotion or often used it in vain, and by their deeds having made themselves unworthy of the name of Christian. In atonement for their sins, I offer you the perfect holiness of your Son, who glorified your name in his preaching and in all his works.

Thy kingdom come. I beg you, O loving Father, to pardon the souls in purgatory for having neither desired nor sincerely sought after your kingdom, in which true rest and eternal glory consist. To expiate all the indifference they have shown, I offer you the fervent desire of Jesus, your Son, that we may all be co-heirs of his kingdom.

Thy will be done on earth, as it is in heaven. I beg you, O loving Father, to pardon the souls in purgatory, especially the souls of religious who during life preferred their will to yours, not always loving your will for them but often following their own preferences. In reparation for their disobedience, I offer you the humble Heart of your Son, which was always united to your holy will, shown in his ready obedience to you even unto death on the Cross.

Give us this day our daily bread. I beg you, O loving Father, to pardon the souls in purgatory for not having received the most holy Sacrament of the altar with the desire, devotion, and love that it merits, or for having made themselves unworthy of it by seldom or never having received it. In atonement for these sins, I offer you the perfect sanctity, devotion, and love of your Son for you, and the ardent love and ineffable desire that compelled him to give us this precious treasure of the Eucharist.

And forgive us our trespasses, as we forgive those who trespass against us. I beg you, O loving Father, to forgive the souls in purgatory for any mortal sins they committed, for all unforgiveness toward those who offended them, and for every failure to love their enemies. For these sins, I offer you the same prayer your Son made upon the Cross for his enemies: "Father, forgive them, for they know not what they do."

And lead us not into temptation. I beg you, O loving Father, to forgive the souls in purgatory for not having fought against their vices and wrongful desires, for having consented to the temptations of the devil and the flesh, and for having willfully given way to bad actions. In expiation for these sins, I offer you the glorious victory of your Son over the world and the devil, his most holy life with its works and fatigue, and his bitter passion and death.

But deliver us and them from every evil and every woe through the merits of your beloved Son, and bring us to the kingdom of your glory, which is none other than your most glorious self. Amen.

Saint Mechtilde of Hackeborn

VI

Recommended Practices on Behalf of the Deceased

"Blessed are the merciful, for they will receive mercy."

Matthew 5:7

There is a beautiful line in the Book of Ruth as Naomi takes leave of her two daughters-in-law and prepares to return to Bethlehem after the death of her sons: "May the Lord deal kindly with you, as you have dealt with the dead and with me" (Ruth 1:8). It is a reminder that our charity toward the deceased is a blessing not only to them but to ourselves as well. The Catholic tradition offers a variety of rich and meaningful practices on behalf of our dearly departed throughout the year and especially in the month of November.

Prayer for the Dead Before Mass

Heavenly Father, your beloved Son, Jesus Christ, instituted the Sacrifice of his Body and Blood for the dead as well as for the living. In union with the most Holy Sacrifice of the Mass, I offer you my humble prayers and beseech you to have mercy on all our brothers and sisters suffering in purgatory. I particularly recommend to your infinite mercy the souls of my parents, relatives, friends, and all those I am connected to in any way, as well as those who suffer the most intense pain, are forgotten by everyone, or for whom you wish me to pray. Mary, compassionate Mother of the Poor Souls, assist me with your powerful intercession. Amen.

Prayer for the Dead at the Offertory

O most compassionate Jesus, have mercy on the souls detained in purgatory, for whose redemption you took upon yourself our nature and endured the bitter death of the Cross. Through the celebration of this most holy Sacrifice and by virtue of your passion, release them from the pains due to their sins. O most merciful Jesus, let your Precious Blood reach down into purgatory and revive the souls who suffer there. Bring them forth into your everlasting light and peace. Amen.

Prayer for the Dead After Mass

May my participation in this most holy Sacrament, I beseech you, Lord, obtain rest and life everlasting for the souls of N. and all those who have died in your peace. Grant that the souls of my family members, relatives, and friends, once purified of all sins by virtue of this Sacrament, may through your mercy receive the reward of eternal joy with you. Amen.

Prayer at a Cemetery

Lord, I recommend to you the soul of N., whose body rests here. May the words of Christ in the Sermon on the Mount become for him/her and for all who rest in this cemetery the Good News of eternal salvation.

May the kingdom of heaven be theirs.
May they possess it as a "Promised Land."
May they have eternal joy.
May they be satisfied in their hunger and thirst
for righteousness.
May they be called your children forever.

May they see you face-to-face.

May their joy and happiness be full and unlimited.

O God, the glory of believers and the life of the just, who saved us by the death and resurrection of your Son, be merciful to our departed brothers and sisters. When they were in our midst, they professed their faith in the resurrection; give them endless bliss. Through Christ, our Lord. Amen.

Adapted from Saint John Paul II[8]

On the Anniversary of Death

We beseech you, O Lord, on this anniversary of the death of N., to grant the soul of your servant companionship with the saints and to pour upon her/him the perennial dew of your love and mercy. Through Christ, our Lord. Amen.

Stations of the Cross

You can pray the Way of the Cross following the images in your church, moving from station to station, or, if that is not possible, by simply gazing at a crucifix and calling to mind each individual station. What is important is to contemplate the great love of Jesus for you and for humanity in undergoing so much suffering and offering his life for our salvation. We suggest that as you accompany Jesus along his sorrowful road to Calvary, you:

— Begin each station with the prayer:

We adore you, O Christ,
and we bless you,
because by your holy Cross
you have redeemed the world.

— Call to mind the station and reflect on it.

— Offer a brief prayer or aspiration, such as the ones provided below.

— End each station, joining yourself to Mary most holy with the prayer:

Holy Mother! Pierce me through;
In my heart each wound renew
Of my Savior crucified.

— Add the invocation:

> Mary, Mother of God and Mother of mercy, pray for us and for the souls of the faithful departed.

— Proceed to the next station.

I Station

Jesus is condemned to death

Jesus Master, although innocent, you are condemned and accept the bitter chalice of crucifixion for love of us. By your passion and death, have pity on the souls in purgatory who are willingly and justly expiating their sins.

II Station

Jesus takes up his cross

Lord Jesus, you take the cross upon your shoulder; through your cross we have been saved. Release from purgatory into your everlasting peace those who walked with you on the Way of the Cross in life and died marked with the sign of faith.

III Station

Jesus falls the first time

Blessed Jesus, even in apparent powerlessness, you are redeeming us! Look with mercy on those who are in purgatory because of sins of weakness and admit them soon into your presence.

IV Station

Jesus meets his afflicted Mother

Most Sorrowful Mother, you never abandon your divine Son but remain at his side always. Be a mother to those being purified in purgatory, especially my own family members and friends.

V Station

Simon of Cyrene helps Jesus carry the cross

Loving Redeemer, Simon's life was changed by this act of compassion. In your mercy, release from purgatory those who sought to alleviate the sufferings of others in life. Let them enjoy eternal bliss and praise you forever.

VI Station

Veronica wipes the face of Jesus

Suffering Jesus, how your face has been disfigured by the tortures you endured! Those who recognize you in the suffering of others are like Veronica. Call to heaven those souls who were most outstanding in their charity toward others, even at the cost of personal sacrifice.

VII Station

Jesus falls the second time

Lord Jesus Christ, our repeated sins and indifference thrust you to the ground once again. Have compassion on those who are in purgatory because of their indifference toward sin; let them experience your generous mercy and admit them soon into their eternal dwelling.

VIII Station

Jesus comforts the women of Jerusalem

Merciful Lord, even in your extreme suffering, your first thought is for others. Impress the charity of your Heart on my heart! Open the gates of heaven to those souls in purgatory who did good to me in life and never let me forget to pray for them.

IX Station

Jesus falls the third time

Divine Savior, insults are heaped upon you as you fall again. Through this third fall, rescue from purgatory those who were rejected and mistreated in life. May their liberation give you great glory.

X Station

Jesus is stripped of his garments

Meek Redeemer, how cruelly you are stripped, your wounded body exposed! Pardon those who are in purgatory because of sins against the body. Through your merits, may they be speedily purified.

XI Station

Jesus is nailed to the cross

Crucified Lord, nailed to the altar of the cross, slain to ransom us from the grip of Satan! Through your agonizing death, may the most abandoned souls in purgatory be released and taken into paradise with you this day.

XII Station

Jesus dies on the cross

Jesus, Son of God, your sacrifice is complete; you, the Innocent One, were immolated to redeem us from our sins. Call from purgatory to heaven those who were most devoted to your passion and to the Holy Mass. Have mercy especially on priests.

XIII Station

Jesus is taken down from the cross

Silent Lord, for a brief time, death seemed to claim you, but you have conquered death and won eternal life for us. In your goodness, raise to glory those souls who in life accompanied others in sickness and death.

XIV Station

Jesus is laid in the tomb

Immortal God, once concealed in the tomb; now concealed under the appearance of bread in our tabernacles: in your love, release from purgatory those souls who kept vigil in adoration before you and let them behold your face forever in eternal life.

℣. Save us, O Christ our Savior, through the power of your Cross.

℟. You who saved Peter on the sea, have mercy on us and on the souls of the faithful departed.

Let us pray.

O God, you sanctified the standard of the life-bestowing Cross with the precious Blood of your only-begotten Son. Grant that those who joyfully honor the holy Cross may everywhere rejoice in your protection. Through the same Christ, our Lord. Amen.

Novena Prayer of Saint Alphonsus Liguori

To be prayed for nine consecutive days.

O most sweet Jesus, through the bloody sweat that you poured out in the Garden of Gethsemane, have mercy on these blessed souls. Have mercy on them.

℟. *Have mercy on them, O Lord.*

O most sweet Jesus, through the pains that you suffered during your most cruel scourging, have mercy on them.

℟. *Have mercy on them, O Lord.*

O most sweet Jesus, through the pains that you suffered in the most painful crowning with thorns, have mercy on them.

℟. *Have mercy on them, O Lord.*

O most sweet Jesus, through the pains that you suffered in carrying the heavy cross to Calvary, have mercy on them.

℟. *Have mercy on them, O Lord.*

O most sweet Jesus, through the pains that you suffered during your most cruel crucifixion, have mercy on them.

℟. *Have mercy on them, O Lord.*

O most sweet Jesus, through the pains that you suffered in your most bitter agony on the cross, have mercy on them.

℟. *Have mercy on them, O Lord.*

O most sweet Jesus, through the immense pain that you suffered in breathing forth your blessed soul to the Father, have mercy on them.

℟. *Have mercy on them, O Lord.*

Blessed souls, I have prayed for you; I beseech you, who are so dear to God and who are sure of never losing him, to pray for us poor sinners, who are in danger of rejecting God and of losing him forever.

Let us pray.

O God, author of mercy and lover of the salvation of humankind, we beseech you on behalf of our brethren, relations, and friends who have departed this life, that through the intercession of the Blessed Virgin Mary and of all the saints, you would receive them soon into the enjoyment of eternal happiness, through Christ our Lord. Amen.

Chaplet of Divine Mercy

This may be prayed using a five-decade rosary.

> Bring to me souls who are in the prison of purgatory and immerse them in the abyss of my mercy.
>
> —*Jesus to Saint Faustina Kowalska*

In this prayer we offer Jesus—Body, Blood, soul, and divinity—to God the Father, and we unite ourselves with his sacrifice offered on the Cross for the salvation of the world. We hand over all our needs and ask for mercy for ourselves and for all people: those living on earth and the souls in purgatory.

Opening Prayers *(optional)*

You expired, Jesus, but the source of life gushed forth for souls, and the ocean of mercy opened up for the whole world. O Fount of Life, unfathomable Divine Mercy, envelop the whole world and empty yourself out upon us.

Repeat three times:

O Blood and Water, which gushed forth from the Heart of Jesus as a fountain of mercy for us, I trust in you!

Begin with an Our Father, Hail Mary, and Apostles' Creed (see *page 113–114).*

On the single bead before each decade:

Eternal Father, I offer you the Body and Blood, soul and divinity of your dearly beloved Son, our Lord Jesus Christ, in atonement for our sins and those of the whole world.

On the ten beads of each decade:

For the sake of his sorrowful passion, have mercy on us and on the whole world.

After the five decades, conclude with:

Holy God, Holy Mighty One, Holy Immortal One, have mercy on us and on the whole world (*three times*).

Closing Prayer *(optional)*

Eternal God, in whom mercy is endless and the treasury of compassion inexhaustible, look kindly upon us and increase your mercy in us, that in difficult moments we might not despair nor become despondent, but with great confidence submit ourselves to your holy will, which is love and mercy itself. Amen.

Saint Faustina Kowalska

Chaplet to Jesus for the Souls in Purgatory

1. Lord, my Creator and Redeemer, I believe that in your justice you established purgatory for those souls who pass into eternity before having totally paid their debts of sin or punishment. I also believe that in your mercy you accept prayers, particularly the Holy Sacrifice of the Mass, for their relief and liberation. Stir up my faith and infuse in my heart sentiments of pity toward these dear suffering brothers and sisters.

Eternal rest . . .

2. Lord Jesus Christ, King of glory, through the intercession of Mary and all the saints, free the souls of the faithful departed from the punishments of purgatory. And through the intercession of Saint Michael, standard-bearer of the heavenly army, guide them to the holy light promised to Abraham and to his descendants. I offer you, Lord, sacrifices and prayers of praise. Accept them for these souls and admit them soon to eternal joy.

Eternal rest . . .

3. Jesus, good Master, I plead with you on behalf of the souls toward whom I have a greater debt of gratitude, justice, charity, and family bonds: parents, spouse, children, brothers and sisters, mentors, relatives, and friends. I recommend to you those who had greater responsibilities on earth, especially religious and civil authorities. I commend especially N. and those souls who have been forgotten by their friends and family members. Lord, admit them soon into eternal happiness.

Eternal rest . . .

4. Jesus, Divine Master, I thank you for having come down from heaven to free us from so many evils by your teaching, holiness, and death. I plead with you on behalf of the souls who are in purgatory because of the media. I have confidence that these souls, once freed from their sufferings and admitted into eternal joy, will supplicate you on behalf of the modern world, so that the many means you have granted us for elevating this earthly life may also be used for making you known and for life everlasting.

Eternal rest . . .

5. Merciful Jesus, by your sorrowful passion and by that love you have for me, I beg you to cancel the punishments that I deserve in this life or in the next because of my many sins. Grant me, O Lord, a spirit of penance, purity of conscience, hatred for every deliberate venial sin, and the dispositions necessary to gain indulgences. I resolve to help the holy souls in purgatory with prayers and good works as much as I can. And you, O infinite Goodness, infuse in me ever greater fervor, so that after death I may be admitted into heaven to contemplate you forever.

Eternal rest . . .

Blessed James Alberione

Prayer of a Hundred Eternal Rests

A rosary may be used to keep count, circling the beads twice.

Place yourself in the presence of God with the Sign of the Cross and pray an act of contrition.

First Decade: My Jesus, for the benefit of the souls in purgatory, I offer you the merits of your sufferings endured for our redemption. I contemplate the blood you shed due to the sadness and anguish you experienced in the Garden of Gethsemane.

Pray ten Eternal Rests.

Holy souls of purgatory, pray to God for me, and may the Father give you the glory of paradise. Amen.

Second Decade: My Jesus, I offer you for the souls of purgatory the immense affliction that oppressed your heart to see that Judas, a disciple whom you loved and favored, became a persecutor, and with a sacrilegious kiss betrayed you, delivering you into the hands of your enemies.

Pray ten Eternal Rests. Holy souls of purgatory . . .

Third Decade: My Jesus, I offer you for the souls of purgatory the admirable patience with which you endured the tortures of the vile soldiers who led you to Annas, Caiaphas, Pilate, and Herod, insulting you and hitting you amid mockeries and insults.

Pray ten Eternal Rests. Holy souls of purgatory . . .

Fourth Decade: My Jesus, I offer you for the souls of purgatory the bitterness you felt when they chose Barabbas, a criminal, over you, the innocent one, and had you tied to a pillar and scourged without mercy.

Pray ten Eternal Rests. Holy souls of purgatory . . .

Fifth Decade: My Jesus, I offer you for the souls of purgatory the humiliation you suffered when, treating you as a mock king, the soldiers put a purple cloak on your shoulders and crowned your head with thorns. In this condition Pilate presented you to the mob, saying, "Look at the man!"

Pray ten Eternal Rests. Holy souls of purgatory . . .

Sixth Decade: My Jesus, I offer you for the souls of purgatory the compassion and deep pain you felt when you were separated violently from your beloved Mother, who came to meet and embrace you on your way to Calvary.

Pray ten Eternal Rests. Holy souls of purgatory . . .

Seventh Decade: My Jesus, I offer you for the souls of purgatory the untold torments you endured when your tortured body was extended on the cross and your hands and feet were nailed to it, and when the cross was raised violently and thrust in the ground.

Pray ten Eternal Rests. Holy souls of purgatory . . .

Eighth Decade: My Jesus, I offer you for the souls of purgatory the tormenting thirst that you suffered on Calvary—thirst for water, but also for souls—and for which you received only vinegar and ingratitude.

Pray ten Eternal Rests. Holy souls of purgatory . . .

Ninth Decade: My Jesus, I offer you for the souls of purgatory the anguish and pains that, for three hours, you endured while hanging on the cross as your Mother stood near you, sharing your agony.

Pray ten Eternal Rests. Holy souls of purgatory . . .

Tenth Decade: My Jesus, I offer you for the souls of purgatory the desolation that your Mother endured when you died and your lifeless body was lowered from the cross and placed in her arms.

Pray ten Eternal Rests. Holy souls of purgatory . . .

Blessed Anna Maria Taigi

All Souls' Day Prayer

Lord Jesus, have mercy on the souls in purgatory. It was for their salvation that you took on our human nature and suffered a most painful death. Have pity on them, on their ardent desire to see you, and on their tears of longing and repentance. Through the merits of your passion, deliver them from the suffering they incurred by their sins.

Loving Jesus, may your blood descend on these dear souls. May it shorten their time of atonement, and may they soon be admitted to eternal happiness in your presence. Amen.

VII

Mary, Gate of Heaven

"Here is your mother."

—*John 19:27*

Mary's loving concern extends not only to her children on earth, but equally to her children in purgatory. She consoles them and alleviates their suffering in the name of her divine Son. Mary intercedes constantly before Jesus for them. With confidence we can entrust our dear departed ones to her, secure in the knowledge that she will be a loving mother to them.

Our Lady revealed herself to Saint Bridget of Sweden as the Mother of all souls in purgatory, adding, "I am Mother of Mercy to these my children who are in the greatest need of my assistance, since in their torments they cannot help themselves." Mary in her sorrows and as Our Lady of Mount Carmel is often invoked to intercede for these souls.

Rosary for the Faithful Departed

The holy Rosary is a most powerful prayer for the liberation of the souls in purgatory. The very words of the Hail Mary remind us that the mother given us by Jesus is full of compassion for all our needs. She will never turn us away or refuse our prayer for our beloved dead.

Begin the Rosary by making the Sign of the Cross; then, pray the Apostles' Creed. On the beads following the crucifix, pray one Our Father, three Hail Marys, and a Glory Be. Next, read the mystery and offer your intention for that mystery, followed by one Our Father, ten Hail Marys, and a Glory Be. It is recommended to then pray the Fatima Prayer and the invocation for the souls in purgatory. All decades are prayed in the same manner, while pondering the mystery and the intention for each decade. Pray the Hail Holy Queen at the end.

Prayers of the Rosary

Sign of the Cross

In the name of the Father, and of the Son, and of the Holy Spirit. Amen.

Apostles' Creed

I believe in God,
the Father almighty,
Creator of heaven and earth,
and in Jesus Christ, his only Son, our Lord,
who was conceived by the Holy Spirit,
born of the Virgin Mary,
suffered under Pontius Pilate,
was crucified, died, and was buried;
he descended into hell;
on the third day he rose again from the dead;
he ascended into heaven,
and is seated at the right hand of God, the Father almighty;
from there he will come to judge the living and the dead.
I believe in the Holy Spirit,
the holy catholic Church,

the Communion of Saints,
the forgiveness of sins,
the resurrection of the body,
and life everlasting. Amen.

Our Father

Our Father,
who art in heaven,
hallowed be thy name;
thy kingdom come;
thy will be done on earth as it is in heaven.
Give us this day our daily bread,
and forgive us our trespasses,
as we forgive those who trespass against us,
and lead us not into temptation,
but deliver us from evil. Amen.

Hail Mary

Hail Mary, full of grace;
the Lord is with thee.
Blessed art thou among women,
and blessed is the fruit of thy womb, Jesus.
Holy Mary, Mother of God,
pray for us sinners,
now and at the hour of our death. Amen.

Glory Be

Glory be to the Father,
and to the Son, and to the Holy Spirit,
as it was in the beginning,
is now, and ever shall be, world without end.
Amen.

Fatima Prayer

O my Jesus, forgive us our sins. Save us from the fires of hell. Lead all souls to heaven, especially those who have most need of your mercy.

Invocation

O Mary, Mother of mercy, console the souls in purgatory, especially those most abandoned.

Hail Holy Queen

Hail, holy Queen, Mother of mercy, our life, our sweetness, and our hope! To you do we cry, poor banished children of Eve. To you do we send up our sighs, mourning, and weeping in this valley of tears. Turn then, most gracious advocate, your eyes of mercy toward us; and after this, our exile, show unto us the blessed fruit of your womb, Jesus. O clement, O loving, O sweet Virgin Mary.

1. The Annunciation of the Angel to Mary (Lk 1:26–38)

Intention: For all the souls being purified in purgatory, especially those whom Jesus and Mary desire to see freed most quickly on account of the intimate relationship they had with them on earth. May heaven soon be theirs!

2. Mary Visits Her Cousin Elizabeth (Lk 1:39–45)

Intention: For the souls of all our deceased parents, relatives, and friends. May those we have loved on earth soon enter the joy of their Creator and Redeemer and rejoice in his love for all eternity.

3. The Birth of Jesus at Bethlehem (Lk 2:1–14)

Intention: For the souls of children and all those who were poor in spirit, relying on the Lord. May our divine Savior shorten their time in purgatory and take them into his wonderful light.

4. The Presentation of Jesus in the Temple (Lk 2:22–38)

Intention: For the souls in purgatory who most yearn to see the face of God. May the Lord in his loving compassion bring them soon into his holy presence.

5. The Finding of the Child Jesus in the Temple (Lk 2:41–51)

Intention: For the souls of those who are in purgatory for having failed to follow God's will. May the Lord show them his mercy and release them soon from their suffering, bringing them to the heavenly homeland awaiting them.

The Luminous Mysteries

1. John Baptizes Jesus in the Jordan (Mt 3:13–17)

Intention: For the souls of all the baptized who are in purgatory, especially those who sought to live their Christian faith sincerely and who inspired others to do the same. May God grant them eternal rest.

2. Jesus Reveals His Glory at the Wedding of Cana (Jn 2:1–11)

Intention: For the souls of those who are in purgatory because of their lack of trust in our divine Lord. May Jesus pour out his mercy and admit them soon to the wedding banquet of heaven.

3. Jesus Proclaims the Kingdom of God and Calls Us to Conversion (Mk 1:14–15)

Intention: For the souls of deceased missionaries and evangelizers, that their sins may soon be expiated, and that they may reap the reward of their labors, to the greater glory of God.

4. The Transfiguration of Jesus (Lk 9:28–36)

Intention: For the souls of consecrated religious and those who were committed to a life of service to the Church. May the Lord shorten their time in purgatory and open to them the gates of heaven, where they may continue to praise and adore him.

5. Jesus Gives Us the Eucharist (Mk 14:22–25)

Intention: For the souls of priests in purgatory, especially those to whom we are indebted for the sacraments and spiritual guidance. May they soon enjoy the company of Jesus, the eternal High Priest.

The Sorrowful Mysteries

1. Jesus Prays in the Garden of Gethsemane (Mk 14:32–42)

Intention: For the most abandoned and forgotten souls in purgatory. May they soon be released from that place of purification into heavenly glory.

2. Jesus Is Scourged (Mk 15:15)

Intention: For the souls in purgatory who were most devoted to the passion of Christ. May his blood alleviate their sufferings and shorten their purification so that they may join him more quickly in paradise.

3. Jesus Is Crowned with Thorns (Mt 27:27–31)

Intention: For the souls of those who are expiating injuries done to others; may they intercede for the healing of their victims and extol God's mercy for all eternity.

4. Jesus Carries the Cross to Calvary (Lk 23:26–32)

Intention: For the souls of those who caused others to sin, especially when this was magnified and multiplied through the means of communication. Once released from purgatory, may they intercede on behalf of media users.

5. Jesus Is Crucified and Dies (Lk 23:33–49; Jn 19:25–27)

Intention: For the souls of all who died for their country or for the sake of others. May Jesus reward their generous, self-sacrificing love, shorten their time of purification, and take them speedily to himself.

The Glorious Mysteries

1. Jesus Rises from the Dead (Mt 28:1–6)

Intention: For the souls of all whom death caught unawares, who died a sudden or unexpected death, that they may speedily rejoice with Jesus in the glory of the resurrection.

2. Jesus Ascends into Heaven (Acts 1:9–11)

Intention: For the souls of all who did good to us while on earth—materially or spiritually, through word or example. May they soon enjoy the eternal vision of God.

3. The Holy Spirit Descends on Mary and the Apostles (Acts 2:1–4)

Intention: For those who are in purgatory because of lukewarmness and indifference in living their faith. May divine Love burn ardently in them so that they may soon enter their heavenly dwelling.

4. Mary Is Assumed into Heaven (see Lk 1:48–49)

Intention: For the souls about to enter heaven; may they intercede for all who struggle to hope and believe in the heavenly reward.

5. Mary Is Crowned Queen of Heaven and Earth (Rev 12:1)

Intention: For those in purgatory who were most devoted to the Blessed Virgin Mary, that they may soon rejoice in her company.

The Memorare

Remember, O most gracious Virgin Mary,
that never was it known that anyone who fled to your protection,
implored your help, or sought your intercession was left unaided.
Inspired with this confidence, I fly to you, O virgin of virgins, my Mother.
To you I come, before you I stand, sinful and sorrowful.
O Mother of the Word Incarnate, despise not my petitions,
but in your mercy, hear and answer me. Amen.

Litany to Our Lady, Help of the Souls in Purgatory

Lord, have mercy on us. *Christ, have mercy on us.*

Lord, have mercy on us. Christ, hear us.
Christ, graciously hear us.

God the Father of heaven,

Response: *Have mercy on the souls of the faithful departed.*

God the Son, Redeemer of the world, ℟.

God the Holy Spirit, ℟.

Holy Trinity, One God, ℟.

Holy Mary,

Response: *Intercede for the souls of the faithful departed.*

Holy Mother of God, ℟.

Our Lady of the Angels, ℟.

Mother of Mount Carmel, ℟.

Mother most merciful, ℟.

Mother of compassion, ℟.

Mother of pity, ℟.

Our Lady of Fatima, ℟.

Our Lady of Lourdes, ℟.

Our Lady of La Salette, ℟.
Our Lady of the Miraculous Medal, ℟.
Our Lady of Ransom, ℟.
Our Lady of Guadalupe, ℟.
Our Lady of Quito, ℟.
Our Lady of Good Counsel, ℟.
Our Lady of the Rosary, ℟.
Our Lady of Perpetual Help, ℟.
Our Lady, Help of Christians, ℟.
Our Lady of Mercy, ℟.
Our Lady of Clemency, ℟.
Our Lady of Tears, ℟.
Our Lady of Victories, ℟.
Beg your Son to spare the souls in purgatory,

Response: *We beseech you, merciful Mother, hear us.*

Beg your Son to deliver the souls in purgatory from all pain, ℟.

Beg your Son to deliver the souls in purgatory from his just punishment, ℟.

Beg your Son to deliver the souls in purgatory from the expiating fire, ℟.

Beg your Son to deliver the souls in purgatory from the shadow of death, ℟.

Beg your Son through your Immaculate Conception to show mercy to the souls in purgatory, ℟.

Beg your Son, through the power of his Nativity, to show mercy to the souls in purgatory, ℟.

Beg your Son, through the power of his most holy name, to show mercy to the souls in purgatory, ℟.

Beg your Son, through the multitude of his tender mercies, to show mercy to the souls in purgatory, ℟.

Beg your Son, through his most bitter passion, to show mercy to the souls in purgatory, ℟.

Beg your Son, through his most sacred wounds, to show mercy to the souls in purgatory, ℟.

Beg your Son, through his most precious Blood, to show mercy to the souls in purgatory, ℟.

Beg your Son, through his cruel death, by which he destroyed death, to show mercy to the souls in purgatory, ℟.

Beg your Son, who absolved the sinful woman and heard the prayer of the good thief, to show mercy to the souls in purgatory, ℟.

Beg your Son to release our deceased parents, relatives, friends, and benefactors from the bonds of their sins and the punishment due them, ℟.

Beg your Son to hasten the day of visiting his faithful departed and to speedily transport them to the heavenly city of eternal peace, ℟.

Beg your Son to shorten the time of expiation for their sins and graciously admit the departed into his holy sanctuary, ℟.

Beg Jesus through your prayers and sufferings, and especially by his inestimable sacrifice on Calvary, renewed in every Mass, to receive the faithful departed into his dwelling and crown their longing with everlasting joy, ℟.

Lamb of God, who takes away the sins of the world, *grant them eternal rest.* (3x)

℣. Christ, hear us.
℟. *Christ, graciously hear us.*
℣. Lord, have mercy on us.
℟. *Christ, have mercy on us.*

Our Father . . .

Let us pray.

O God, Creator and Redeemer of all the faithful, grant the souls of your departed servants the remission of all their sins, that through our prayerful supplications they may obtain the pardon that they have desired. Through the merits of Jesus Christ, our Lord, and the intercession of his most holy Mother. Amen.

Hail Mary for the Souls in Purgatory

Hail Mary. Behold, most merciful Mother, your poor and sorrowful children who suffer so grievously in the purification of purgatory. We beg you, for the sake of the great joy which the angelic salutation gave you, to have compassion on them and send them your holy angel to bring them a joyful greeting and release from their sufferings.

Full of grace. Obtain for them grace, mercy, and remission of the great cleansing they now endure.

The Lord is with thee. He will deny you nothing but will hear your prayer and mercifully come to the assistance of these dear souls.

Blessed art thou among women. Yes, among all creatures in the world! Bless and render the souls in purgatory happy through your intercession, delivering them from their bonds.

And blessed is the fruit of thy womb, Jesus, who is the Savior and Redeemer of the whole world, born of you, a virgin. Have mercy on the departed souls. O loving Mother, hasten to their assistance.

Holy Mary, Mother of God. Wonderful Virgin Mother, *pray for us sinners* and for the souls in purgatory *now* and forever, *and at the hour of our death*; and as you assisted the departed in their last agony, so assist them now in their purification, that, delivered by your motherly intercession, they may pass from their present suffering to everlasting joy, and rejoice with you and the whole heavenly host through all eternity. Amen.

To Our Lady of Intercession

Most holy Mary, Our Lady of Intercession, your maternal tenderness gathers in one embrace all the souls redeemed by the precious Blood of your Son, Jesus. As we remember those who have gone before us, we come before you with unlimited confidence in your intercession. Death has not destroyed the affection that binds us to those who lived in the same faith as we do. O Mary, countless souls in that place of expiation await the assistance of our prayers and the merits of our good works. Urged by the charity of Jesus Christ, we raise our faces and hearts in supplication to you, the compassionate Mother of all believers, in favor of these suffering souls. Make our prayers efficacious, O Mary; let them move the Heart of Jesus, our Redeemer, through your motherly intercession.

Let your incomparable holiness supply the defects of our sinfulness, your love make good our languid affection, your power strengthen our weakness. Grant, O Queen of Heaven, that the ardent desire of the souls of the departed to be admitted to the beatific vision may soon be satisfied. We pray to you, O Mother, especially for the souls of our relatives, of priests, of those who were faithful in honoring you, of those who did good to others, of those who wept with others and for them, and, finally, for the souls of those who are most forgotten. Grant that one day, when we are all reunited in heaven, we may be able to rejoice in the possession of God, in the happiness of your dear presence, and in the fellowship of all the saints, thanking you, dear Mother, who are our unfailing comfort, for all the blessings you have obtained for us. Amen.

To Our Lady of Sorrows

Most Blessed Virgin Mary, Mother of Sorrows, I turn to you in supplication. By the sword that pierced your heart as you stood under the cross of your beloved Son, I pray and ask you to help the holy souls in purgatory, and particularly N., for whom I now pray. O Mother of Sorrows and Refuge of Sinners, through your powerful intercession and for the love of your divine Son, whose precious Blood was shed for us, I beg you to release from purgatory those who most deserve your compassion. Help the living who are in danger of falling into sin. Pray for us, Mother of mercy, now and at the hour of our death. May we one day rejoice with you forever in heaven. Amen.

To Our Lady of Mount Carmel

O Lord, you are so merciful. As such, you've created purgatory, a place where we can be cleansed and purified of the lasting effects of our sins.

O Mary, Our Lady of Mount Carmel, you told Saint Simon that you would descend to purgatory each week and release all those who wore your scapular during their lifetime. I pray today on behalf of all the holy souls in purgatory. Please bring them quickly to our Lord. Intercede for them before your Son; I know he will not refuse your request. Release them from their bondage and usher them home to our Lord. There, they can love him and be joyful with him and with you for eternity.

I ask that you particularly watch over any souls in purgatory that I may know and love, especially those of my family and friends. Please also keep in mind my intentions: (*state them here*).

Our Lady of Mount Carmel, pray for us!

Mary, Gate of Heaven

O Mary, gate of heaven,
mirror of divine light,
tabernacle of the covenant
between God and humanity,
grant that our souls may fly to you
when they take leave of this earth.
Let them rise,
following the radiant path
you have traced for us,
transported by a hope
that the world cannot give:
the hope of heavenly beatitude.

O Mother most merciful,
comfort us from heaven,
and, through your examples of purity and hope,
one day lead us and the souls of all our dearly departed

to the blessed encounter with you
and with your Son,
our Savior, Jesus Christ.[9]

Adapted from Saint Paul VI

Novena to God Through Mary for the Souls in Purgatory

The intentions suggested may be replaced, or others added.

℣. O Lord, hear my prayer;
℟. And let my cry come to you.

Opening Prayer

O Heavenly Father, whose mercy fills heaven and earth, be merciful to the poor souls in purgatory. You created each one of them in your own image and likeness and gave them your only-begotten Son for their salvation. On their behalf and in union with your Son, who offers his precious Blood in atonement for their sins, I unite myself to every Sacrifice of the Mass being celebrated at this time, that they may be washed clean and freed from their suffering. It is in this spirit that I offer this novena for their liberation.

First Day

Opening Prayer: O Heavenly Father . . .

Holy, Triune God, receive my prayers and supplications for the Holy Souls, for whom I make this novena; today I especially pray for the soul whose liberation would give you the greatest glory. Through the prayers of Mary most holy, who followed Jesus on the way to Calvary, receive this soul into your loving embrace.

Our Father, Hail Mary, Glory Be, Eternal Rest.

O Mother most merciful, pray for the souls in purgatory!

Second Day

Opening Prayer: O Heavenly Father . . .

Holy, Triune God, receive my prayers and supplications for the Holy Souls, for whom I make this novena; today I especially pray for the soul who is most abandoned and forgotten. Through the prayers of Mary most holy, who suffered with Jesus as he was nailed to the cross, receive this soul into your loving embrace.

Our Father, Hail Mary, Glory Be, Eternal Rest.

O Mother most merciful, pray for the souls in purgatory!

Third Day

Opening Prayer: O Heavenly Father . . .

Holy, Triune God, receive my prayers and supplications for the Holy Souls, for whom I make this novena; today I especially pray for the soul who is undergoing the greatest suffering. Through the prayers of Mary most holy, who with Jesus endured the mockery and insults of his crucifiers, receive this soul into your loving embrace.

Our Father, Hail Mary, Glory Be, Eternal Rest.

O Mother most merciful, pray for the souls in purgatory!

Fourth Day

Opening Prayer: O Heavenly Father . . .

Holy, Triune God, receive my prayers and supplications for the Holy Souls, for whom I make this novena; today I especially pray for the soul who has been the longest in purgatory. Through the prayers of Mary most holy, who received us as her children during the agony of her divine Son, receive this soul into your loving embrace.

Our Father, Hail Mary, Glory Be, Eternal Rest.

O Mother most merciful, pray for the souls in purgatory!

Fifth Day

Opening Prayer: O Heavenly Father . . .

Holy, Triune God, receive my prayers and supplications for the Holy Souls, for whom I make this novena; today I especially pray for the soul who prayed the most for the deceased. Through the prayers of Mary most holy, whose heart was wrenched by Jesus' cry to the Father, "Why have you abandoned me?" receive this soul into your loving embrace.

Our Father, Hail Mary, Glory Be, Eternal Rest.

O Mother most merciful, pray for the souls in purgatory!

Sixth Day

Opening Prayer: O Heavenly Father . . .

Holy, Triune God, receive my prayers and supplications for the Holy Souls, for whom I make this novena; today I especially pray for the soul who was most wounded by the bad example or malice of others. Through the prayers of Mary most holy, whose own heart was pierced when the soldier thrust the lance into the side of her Son, receive this soul into your loving embrace.

Our Father, Hail Mary, Glory Be, Eternal Rest.

O Mother most merciful, pray for the souls in purgatory!

Seventh Day

Opening Prayer: O Heavenly Father . . .

Holy, Triune God, receive my prayers and supplications for the Holy Souls, for whom I make this novena; today I especially pray for the soul who practiced the greatest kindness and goodness while on earth. Through the prayers of Mary most holy, who received the tortured body of her dead Son into her arms, receive this soul into your loving embrace.

Our Father, Hail Mary, Glory Be, Eternal Rest.

O Mother most merciful, pray for the souls in purgatory!

Eighth Day

Opening Prayer: O Heavenly Father . . .

Holy, Triune God, receive my prayers and supplications for the Holy Souls, for whom I make this novena; today I especially pray for the soul who was most devoted to you and to the passion and death of Jesus. Through the prayers of Mary most holy, who laid her lifeless Son in the tomb and watched it being sealed, receive this soul into your loving embrace.

Our Father, Hail Mary, Glory Be, Eternal Rest.

O Mother most merciful, pray for the souls in purgatory!

Ninth Day

Opening Prayer: O Heavenly Father . . .

Holy, Triune God, receive my prayers and supplications for the Holy Souls, for whom I make this novena; today I especially pray for the soul who was most surrendered to your divine will. Through the prayers of Mary most holy, who awaited with trusting hope the resurrection of Jesus, receive this soul into your loving embrace.

Our Father, Hail Mary, Glory Be, Eternal Rest.

O Mother most merciful, pray for the souls in purgatory!

In Honor of Mary's Seven Sorrows

1. Hail Mary, most humble handmaid of the Blessed Trinity! Remember the sufferings you endured in soul and body when your beloved Son shed his precious Blood for us on the eighth day after his birth. Through these sufferings, we beseech you, intercede with God for us sinners and for the souls in purgatory, that they may be delivered from all their sufferings.

Our Father, Hail Mary.

2. Hail Mary, chosen from all eternity, most holy daughter of God the Father! Remember the sufferings you endured in soul and body when you were warned to take flight before the wrath of Herod and to go with your divine Son into the land of Egypt, an exile from your country. Through these sufferings, we beseech you, intercede with God for us sinners and for the souls in purgatory, that they may be delivered from all their sufferings.

Our Father, Hail Mary.

3. Hail Mary, most worthy Mother of Jesus Christ, the Son of God! Remember the sufferings you endured in soul and body when you sought your lost

Son for three days. Through these sufferings, we beseech you, intercede with God for us and for the souls in purgatory, that they may be delivered from all their sufferings.

Our Father, Hail Mary.

4. Hail Mary, most beloved spouse of the Holy Spirit! Remember the sufferings you endured in soul and body when your divine Son took leave of you and told you that he must suffer death on the cross for the sins of the world. Through these sufferings, we beseech you, intercede with God for us sinners and for the souls in purgatory, that they may be delivered from all their sufferings.

Our Father, Hail Mary.

5. Hail Mary, most beautiful Queen of the holy angels! Remember the sufferings you endured in soul and body when you heard that your divine Son was condemned to death and when you saw him carrying the cross upon his wounded shoulders to the place of crucifixion. Through these sufferings, we beseech you, intercede with God for us sinners and for the souls in purgatory, that they may be delivered from all their sufferings.

Our Father, Hail Mary.

6. Hail Mary, glorious Queen of the patriarchs! Remember the sufferings you endured in soul and body when your divine Son was nailed to the cross and when you beheld him hanging upon the cross in unspeakable pain until he gave up his soul. Through these sufferings, we beseech you, intercede with God for us sinners and for the souls in purgatory, that they may be delivered from all their sufferings.

Our Father, Hail Mary.

7. Hail Mary, Mother of the Messiah foretold by the prophets and most anxiously awaited! Remember the sufferings you endured in soul and body when your divine Son was taken from the cross, placed in your arms, and finally laid in the tomb. Through these sufferings, we beseech you, intercede with God for us and for the souls in purgatory, that they may be delivered from all their sufferings. Amen.

Our Father, Hail Mary.

In Honor of Mary's Seven Joys

1. Hail Mary, counsellor of the apostles! Remember the joy you experienced in soul and body when the Archangel Gabriel saluted you and announced the incarnation of your divine Son. Through this joy, we

beseech you, intercede with God for us sinners and for the souls in purgatory, that they may be delivered and attain the eternal joy of heaven.

Our Father, Hail Mary.

2. Hail Mary, teacher of the evangelists! Remember the joy you experienced in soul and body when, without violation of your holy virginity, you gave birth at Bethlehem to your divine Son. Through this joy, we beseech you, intercede with God for us sinners and for the souls in purgatory, that they may be delivered and attain the eternal joy of heaven.

Our Father, Hail Mary.

3. Hail Mary, comforter of the martyrs! Remember the joy you experienced in soul and body when the three holy kings made their worthy offerings to your divine Son and adored him as their true God. Through this joy, we beseech you, intercede with God for us sinners and for the souls in purgatory, that they may be delivered and attain the eternal joy of heaven.

Our Father, Hail Mary.

4. Hail Mary, wise instructor of doctors and confessors! Remember the joy you experienced in soul and body when, after three days, you found your Son

again in the Temple. Through this joy, we beseech you, intercede with God for us sinners and for the souls in purgatory, that they may be delivered and attain the eternal joy of heaven.

Our Father, Hail Mary.

5. Hail Mary, most beautiful jewel of all holy women and virgins! Remember the joy you experienced in soul and body when, on Easter day, your divine Son appeared to you after his glorious resurrection and with filial love greeted and consoled you. Through this joy, we beseech you, intercede with God for us sinners and for the souls in purgatory, that they may be delivered and attain the eternal joy of heaven.

Our Father, Hail Mary.

6. Hail Mary, shining crown of all the saints of God! Remember the joy you experienced in soul and body when your divine Son, by his own power, ascended gloriously into heaven in the presence of his beloved disciples. Through this joy, we beseech you, intercede with God for us sinners and for the souls in purgatory, that they may be delivered and attain the eternal joy of heaven.

Our Father, Hail Mary.

7. Hail Mary, most willing helper and consoler of the living and the dead! Remember the joy you experienced in soul and body when your divine Son invited you to the bliss of heaven, and at the end of your earthly life introduced your glorious soul and body into heaven, placing you above all the choirs of angels. Through this joy, we beseech you, intercede with God for us sinners and for the souls in purgatory, that they may be delivered and attain the eternal joy of heaven. Amen.

Our Father, Hail Mary.

VIII

Preparing for Heaven

Make us know the shortness of life
that we may gain wisdom of heart.
—*See Psalm 90:12*

Literature and the arts through the ages attest to the human yearning for everlasting life and eternal joy. Scripture confirms that God, in his infinite love, created us in his image and likeness and sent his own beloved Son to redeem us so that we could enjoy life with him forever (see Gen 1:27 and Jn 3:16). Still, God leaves us free. Every day we are deciding our future and moving toward eternity. This should not be a cause for anxiety, but rather for trust in God's divine assistance. We can do nothing by ourselves, but with God all things are possible. Nurturing a relationship with the Lord through prayer and a sacramental life will direct our lives toward heaven and give us a small taste even now of the joy of living in union with our Creator and Lord.

Let us pray always for the gift of perseverance, a good death, everlasting life, and the shortest time in purgatory possible, placing our trust in the promise of Jesus, our Savior: "Do not be afraid; I am with you. Whatever you ask in my name, I will do" (see Mt 10:31; 28:20; Jn 14:14).

Means to Grow in Relationship with God and Shorten Purgatory

It is not by their own power that these means are efficacious, but because through them our Lord chooses to apply the fruits of his saving redemption.

- Devotion to the Holy Eucharist: faithful participation at Mass, devout reception of Holy Communion, visits to the most Blessed Sacrament
- Daily reading of Sacred Scripture, especially the New Testament
- Regular reception of the sacrament of Reconciliation
- Devotion to the passion of Jesus Christ, including the Stations of the Cross

- Forgiveness of others
- Doing good to others
- Daily examination of conscience
- Surrender to the will of God
- Purity of intention in words and deeds
- Beginning and ending the day with prayer
- Devotion to Divine Mercy and the Nine First Fridays
- Consecration to the Sacred Heart of Jesus and the Immaculate Heart of Mary
- Devotion to the Blessed Virgin Mary, especially the daily Rosary
- Friendship with the angels and saints, especially our guardian angel, our patron saints, and Saint Joseph
- Offering Masses for our deceased and praying for the holy souls in purgatory
- Fasting and almsgiving
- Asking God to let us expiate our sins on this earth
- Daily prayers for a good death for ourselves and for all the dying

Invocations for a Holy Death

Jesus, Mary, and Joseph, I give you my heart and my soul.
Jesus, Mary, and Joseph, assist me in my last agony.
Jesus, Mary, and Joseph, may I breathe forth my soul in peace with you.

For Perseverance Until Death

Oh, my Lord and Savior, support me in that hour in the strong arms of your sacraments and by the fresh fragrance of your consolations. Let the absolving words be said over me, and the holy oil sign and seal me, and your own Body be my food, and your Blood my sprinkling; and let my sweet Mother, Mary, breathe on me, and my angel whisper peace to me, and my glorious Saints (N. N.) smile upon me; that in them all and through them all, I may receive the gift of perseverance and die, as I desire to live, in your faith, in your Church, in your service, and in your love. Amen.

Saint John Henry Newman

To God Our Father

O God, great and omnipotent judge of the living and the dead,
we are to appear before you after this short life
to render an account of our works.
Give us the grace to prepare for our last hour
by a devout and holy life,
and protect us against sudden death.
Let us remember our frailty and mortality,
that we may always live in the ways of your commandments.
Teach us to be watchful in prayer,
that when your summons come
for our departure from this world,
we may go forth to meet you,
experience a merciful judgment,
and rejoice in everlasting happiness.
We ask this through Christ, our Lord. Amen.

Suscipe

Take, Lord, and receive all my liberty,
my memory, my understanding,
and my entire will,
all I have and call my own.

You have given all to me.
To you, Lord, I return it.
Everything is yours; do with it what you will.
Give me only your love and your grace;
that is enough for me.

Saint Ignatius of Loyola

To Jesus for Protection

O Lord Jesus Christ, let me confess your name with my last breath. In your great mercy receive me and do not disappoint me in my hope. Open the gates of life for me and let the prince of darkness have no power over me. Protect me by your kindness, shield me with your might, and lead me by your right hand to the place of refreshment, the dwelling you have prepared for your servants and for those who revere you. Amen.

Prayer for Mercy

O my Lord and Savior, be merciful to me now that my life is approaching its end and the evening awaits me. My sins are so many. Heal me while I am still on earth, and I shall truly be whole. In your mercy, move me to repent so that I shall not be ashamed when I encounter you in heaven. Amen.

To Jesus Crucified

O Jesus,
while I remember your dying breath,
I beg you to receive mine.
Since I do not know
whether I shall have command of my senses
when I leave this world,
I offer you now my last sufferings
and all the sorrows of my passing.
I give my soul into your hands,
for you are my Lord and my Savior.
Grant that the last beat of my heart
may be an act of perfect love for you. Amen.

Anima Christi

Soul of Christ, sanctify me.
Body of Christ, save me.
Blood of Christ, inebriate me.
Water from Christ's side, wash me.
Passion of Christ, strengthen me.
O good Jesus, hear me.

Within your wounds hide me.
Permit me not to be separated from you.
From the malignant enemy, defend me.
In the hour of my death, call me
and bid me come to you,
that with your saints I may praise you
forever and ever. Amen.

Lead My Soul to Heaven

Most holy Virgin Mary,
always present before the Most Holy Trinity,
and to whom it is granted at all times
to pray for us to your most blessed Son,
pray for me in all my needs.
Help me, defend me, give thanks for me,
and obtain for me the pardon of all my sins and failings.
Help me especially in my last hours.
Then, when I can no longer give any sign of the use of reason,
give me courage and protect me against all evil spirits.
Make in my name a profession of faith.
Assure me of my eternal salvation.

Never let me despair of the mercy of God.
When I can no longer say "Jesus, I place my soul
in your hands,"
say it for me, dear Mother.
When I can no longer hear human words of
consolation,
bring me comfort.
Stay with me when I stand in judgment before
your Son,
and should I be purified in purgatory,
pray for me after my death,
that I may quickly gain the happiness
of being in the presence of God.
Lead my soul to heaven, where, united with you
and all the saints,
I may bless and praise our God for all eternity.
Amen.

To Saint Joseph for a Happy Death

Saint Joseph, protector of the dying, I ask you to intercede for all the dying, and I invoke your assistance in the hour of my own death. You merited a happy passing by a holy life, and in your last hours you had the great consolation of being assisted by

Jesus and Mary. Deliver me from sudden death; obtain for me the grace to imitate you in life, to detach my heart from everything worldly, and daily to gather treasures for the moment of my death. Obtain for me the grace to receive the sacrament of the sick well, and with Mary, fill my heart with sentiments of faith, hope, love, and sorrow for sins, so that I may breathe forth my soul in peace. Amen.

Blessed James Alberione

To My Guardian Angel

My guardian angel, you are always near me, inspiring me to choose the good and strengthening me in the battle against Satan and the forces of evil. Keep me always aware of your presence and mindful of your inspirations. Be with me especially at the last moment of my life. Do not leave me, I beg you, until you see me safe in heaven, praising God and singing his mercies for all eternity. Amen.

Acknowledgements

Papal and magisterial texts copyright © Dicastero per la Comunicazione-Libreria Editrice Vaticana. All rights reserved. Used with permission.

The English translation of the "The Apostles' Creed" by the English Language Liturgical Consultation.

Excerpts from the *Diary*, by St. Faustina Kowalska used with permission of the Marian Fathers of the Immaculate Conception of the Blessed Virgin Mary. Stockbridge, MA.

Excerpt from *Prayers for a Lifetime*, by Karl Rahner used with permission of The Crossroad Publishing Company. Pearl River, NY.

"Prayer in Time of Suicide" from *Tears of God: Persevering in the Face of Great Sorrow or Catastrophe* by Benedict Groeschel used with permission of Ignatius Press. San Francisco, CA.

Every effort has been made to trace copyright holders and to obtain their permission for the use of copyright material. The publisher apologizes for any errors or omissions in the above list and would be grateful if notified of any corrections that should be incorporated in future reprints or editions of this book.

Notes

1. Pope Benedict XVI, *Spe Salvi* (Boston: Pauline Books & Media, 2007), no. 47.

2. Found in most Breviaries or online.

3. To learn more about indulgences, you can visit the Vatican's website to read the Apostolic Constitution of Pope Paul VI, *Indulgen-tiarum Doctrina*, On the doctrine of indulgences for our time, https://www.vatican.va/content/paul-vi/en/apost_constitutions/documents/hf_p-vi_apc_01011967_indulgentiarum-doctrina.html.

4. See Apostolic Penitentiary, *The Gift of the Indulgence*, Rome, January 29, 2000, nos. 3–5, https://www.vatican.va/roman_curia/tribunals/apost_penit/documents/rc_trib_appen_pro_20000129_indulgence_en.html.

5. Pope John Paul II, *Letter of His Holiness Pope John Paul II for the Celebration of the Millennium of the Commemoration of All the Faithful Departed*, June 2, 1998, https://www.vatican.va/content/john-paul-ii/en/letters/1998/documents/hf_jp-ii_let_19980602_cluny.html.

6. Karl Rahner, *Prayers for a Lifetime*, (New York: The Crossroad Publishing Company, 1987), 148–49.

7. Benedict Groeschel, *Tears of God: Persevering in the Face of Great Sorrow or Catastrophe* (San Francisco: Ignatius Press, 2009), 82.

8. Pope John Paul II "Discourse at the Cemetery of Verano," Rome, November 1, 198, https://www.vatican.va/content/john-paul-ii/it/speeches/1981/november/documents/hf_jp-ii_spe_19811101_verano.html, translated by the author.

9. Saint Paul VI, *Preghiamo con Paolo VI*, (Figlie di San Paolo, 2014), p. 146, translated and adapted by the author.

List of Contributors

All prayers were taken from common sources, apart from the following:

Blessed James Alberione, SSP

Chaplet to Jesus for the Souls in Purgatory

Covenant Prayer

To Saint Joseph for a Happy Death

Saint Gertrude of Helfta

Heroic Act of Love

Offering of Christ's Passion

Prayer of Saint Gertrude

Benedict Groeschel, CFR

Prayer in Time of Suicide

Saint Ignatius of Antioch

Second-Century Prayer for the Dead

Saint Ignatius of Loyola

Suscipe

Saint John Chrysostom

Byzantine Prayer for the Deceased

Saint John Paul II

Prayer at a Cemetery

Saint Faustina Kowalska

Chaplet of Divine Mercy

Saint Alphonsus Liguori

Novena Prayer

Blessed Mary of Providence

Remember Us

Saint Mechtilde of Hackeborn

The Lord's Prayer for the Departed

Saint John Henry Newman

For Perseverance Until Death

Saint Nicholas of Tolentino

The Seven Days Prayer for the Dead

Saint Odilo of Cluny

I Promise Never to Forget You

Saint Paul VI

Mary, Gate of Heaven

Karl Rahner, SJ

Let Me Never Forget

A mission of the Daughters of St. Paul

As apostles of Jesus Christ,
evangelizing today's world:

We are CALLED to holiness
by God's living Word and Eucharist.

We COMMUNICATE the Gospel message
through our lives and through all
available forms of media.

We SERVE the Church
by responding to the hopes and needs
of all people with the Word of God,
in the spirit of St. Paul.

For more information visit us at:
www.pauline.org